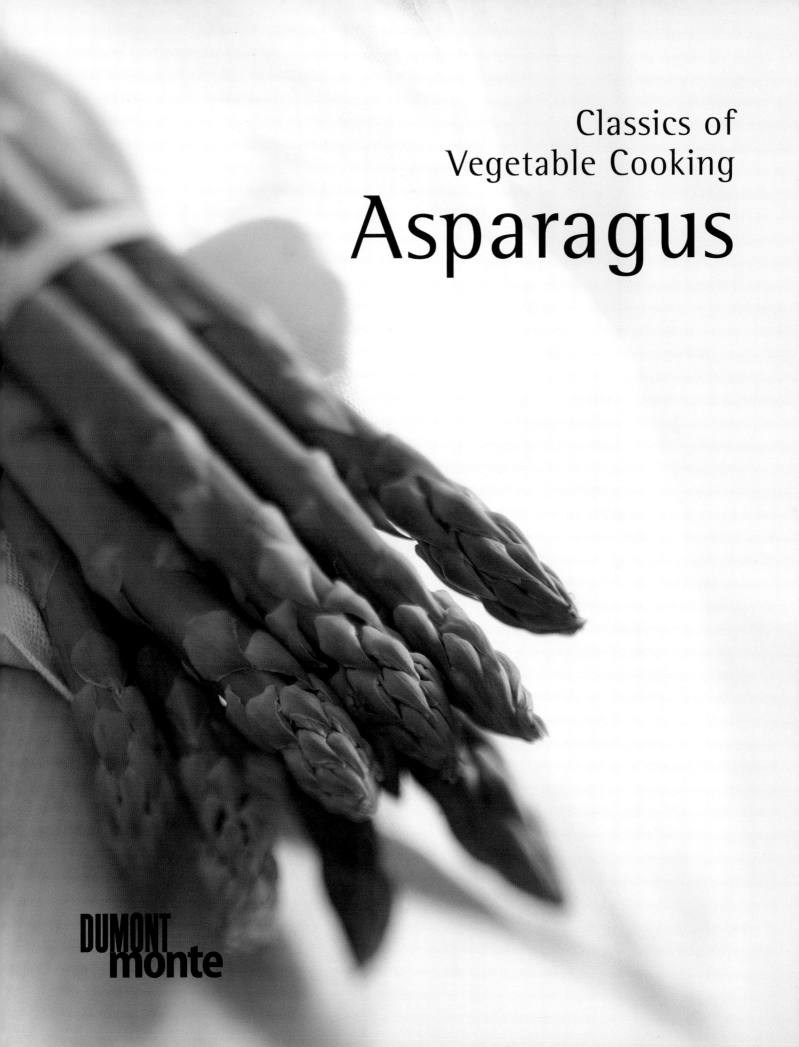

Classics of
Vegetable Cooking
Asparagus

DUMONT
monte

Concept and execution: Meidenbauer • Martin Verlagsbüro, Munich
Text and recipes: Lena Raab
Editorial: Matthias Edbauer, Susanne Maß, Simone Steger, Dr. Carla Meyer
Layout and typesetting: Hubert Grafik Design, Munich
Photography: Brigitte Sporrer, Alena Hrbkova
Food styling: Hans Gerlach
Cover design: BOROS, Wuppertal
© cover photograph: Stock Food (Susi Eising)
Printing: Druckerei Appl, Wemding

© 2001 DuMont Buchverlag, Köln
Dumont monte UK, London
All rights reserved

ISBN 3-7701-7046-6

Printed in Germany

General hints

Eggs: If not otherwise stated, the eggs used in these recipes are of medium size. Eggs should not be eaten raw, particularly by babies, toddlers, pregnant women and old people, and it is strongly advised that any dish using raw eggs should be eaten immediately.

Milk: If not otherwise stated, milk used in these recipes is whole milk (3.5% fat content).

Poultry: Poultry should always be cooked right through before eating. You can tell if it is done by piercing it with a skewer. If the juices run out pink, then it is not ready and must be cooked for a longer time. If the juices are clear then the bird is done.

Nuts: Some of these recipes contain nuts or nut oil. People who have allergies or who tend to be allergic should avoid eating these dishes.

Herbs: If not otherwise stated, these recipes call for fresh herbs. If you cannot obtain these, the amounts in the recipes can be replaced with half the quantity of dried herbs.

Alcohol: Some of the recipes in this book contain alcohol. These dishes should not be served to children or sufferers from alcoholism.

The temperatures and times in these recipes are based on using a conventional oven. If you are using a fan oven, please follow the manufacturer's instructions.

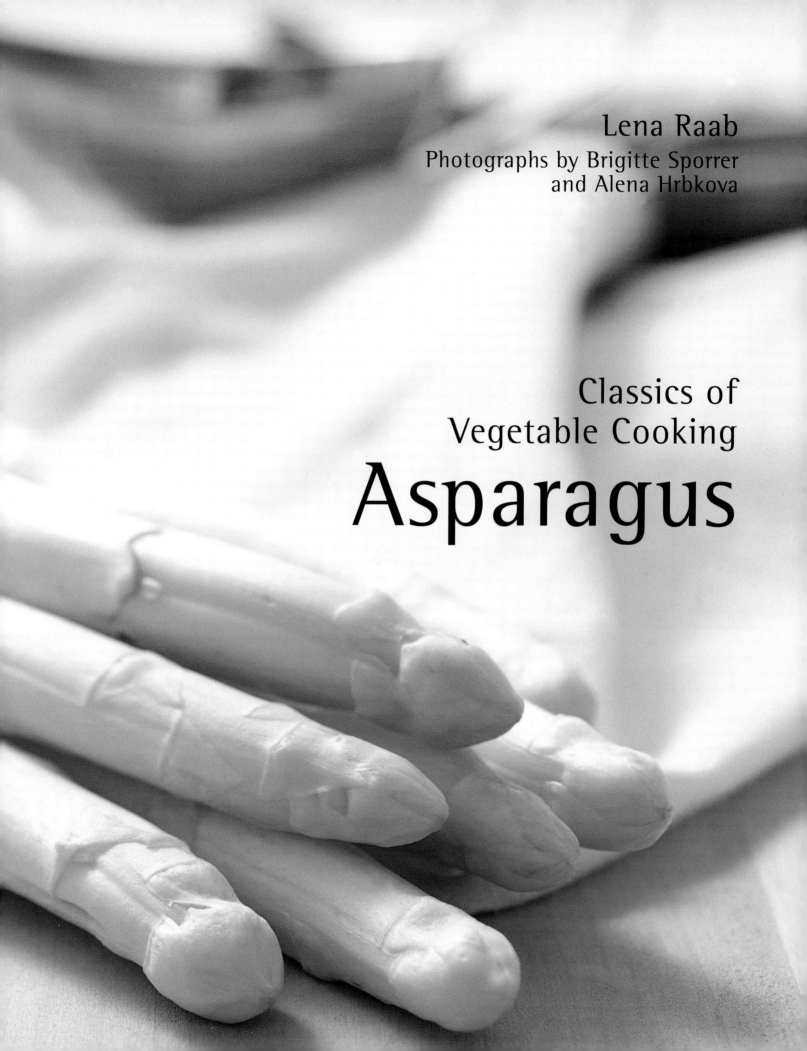

Lena Raab
Photographs by Brigitte Sporrer
and Alena Hrbkova

Classics of
Vegetable Cooking
Asparagus

Contents

Introduction

Nature offers one of its choicest delicacies, asparagus, quite early in the year. Asparagus is a vegetable that can be used to prepare a wide range of delicious dishes, ranging from elaborate recipes to hot and cold snacks, salads and soups. People who enjoy soufflés, vegetable flans and gratins will not be disappointed either. Hardly any other vegetable is so versatile as both green and white asparagus, which can be cooked in a variety of ways and combined with a wide range of foods such potatoes, rice or noodles, meat, fish and cheese, and different kinds of pastry, such as pizza, shortcrust and puff pastry.

Asparagus is a vegetable which is appreciated all over the world and there are countless recipes and ways of using it that add to its attraction. Whether combined with fish from the North Sea, spices and vegetables from the Near and Far East, or influenced by the cuisines of the southern and western parts of the world, asparagus dishes are invariably mouthwatering delicacies.

Asparagus: a harbinger of spring

In France and Germany, white asparagus is inseparable from nature's awakening, the arrival of spring and the first warm sunshine, even in northern latitudes. But in warmer regions, it is the green asparagus that is the harbinger of spring. In southern Europe, for instance, where it is cultivated mainly in Greece, Spain and Italy it can be found even earlier on the market. Later in the season, both kinds appear all over Europe, including in Great Britain, and the vegetable is also grown in the United States. Imported asparagus flown in by air is available almost everywhere.

Asparagus has conquered the world and it makes frequent appearances in restaurant menus, as well as being eaten often at home. In dietary cuisine it has long considered a valuable addition since it is high in vitamins and low in calories. Both green and white asparagus have been cultivated since ancient times, and they have a long, eventful history.

Historically, a noble vegetable

Asparagus will grow in most regions that have a mild climate and a sandy soil. It originated in the Middle East from where it soon spread to China, Egypt and Greece. According to historical evidence, asparagus was already known in Egypt 3000 years ago where it grew as a wild vegetable and was considered a great delicacy. In Greece where it has been documented as far back as 2000 years ago, it was considered a medicinal plant, particularly appreciated for its purifying and purgative properties. For these reasons, asparagus is still used in many diets for losing weight and diets for diabetics.

The Romans were more pleasure-loving than the Greeks and it was they who discovered the culinary aspects of asparagus. They began to cultivate it, growing it in large fields, and they brought it with them to the European countries they conquered.

This is when asparagus began to be cultivated in the milder climate of the regions along the Main, the Rhine and the Danube – in fact, in many of the same regions where it is still cultivated today. After the break-up of the Roman Empire, the cultivation of asparagus completely disappeared, as a result of the wars between the various Germanic tribes and the turmoil resulting from the migration of peoples. For a time, asparagus only occurred as a wild plant in Euorpe.

The convents and monasteries which developed with the spread of Christianity soon became the mainspring of Europe's Christian and cultural life. The monks breathed new life into old traditions and began to cultivate long-forgotten vegetables, herbs and medicinal plants. Asparagus was one the plants that were grown within the confines of these monasteries. The monks and friars were well aware of the noble character of asparagus and they knew that it was not cultivated outside the walls of their monasteries. It was only at the beginning of the 17th century that the kings and monarchs of Europe became aware of asparagus as a great delicacy and started to grow it in the large kitchen gardens and parks of their castles and palaces. Asparagus was experiencing a revival and conquering the world again. Today, it can be found everywhere with a mild climate and a sandy soil, and it is grown extensively throughout Europe and the United States.

White asparagus – green asparagus

Asparagus belongs to the lily family, *Liliaceae*. It has a vigorous rootstock that spreads horizontally through the soil. Asparagus cannot be harvested until three or

four years after planting. Then for a period of 15 to 20 years, the rootstock produces up to six fine shoots every year which grow toward the surface. Fields of asparagus are very distinctive with their earthed-up rows stretching through the countryside like low mountain ranges. This is done because it is the only way for white asparagus to retain its white colour. Indeed, as soon as the asparagus has worked its way up to the light, it soon changes colour – first to lilac and violet, then green. In order to prevent this the asparagus is earthed up and harvested very early in the morning. However, in recent years asparagus is beginning to be harvested when green, an innovation which originated in Italy, Greece and Spain and has spread to our country. But in Germany, white asparagus is the most cultivated kind and still dominates the market and menus. White asparagus has a more delicate aroma than green asparagus but the latter is higher in vitamins and has a more intense flavour. It is particularly suited for dishes combined ingredients with a stronger or spicy flavour.

Asparagus seasons

In Europe, the asparagus season runs from March in the most favourable regions until towards the end of June; St John's Day, 24 June, is traditionally the last day of the asparagus harvest, a date observed by many growers. There is an important reason for this; the plants must be allowed to rest in order to produce the next season's asparagus.

But people who enjoy eating asparagus throughout the year will find it in many shops, flown in from almost everywhere in the world, including southern Europe, the United States, South America and South Africa. In fact, a plate of fresh asparagus for Christmas dinner would present no problem.

Buying and storing asparagus

It is best to buy freshly harvested asparagus. Asparagus is available in many shops and markets and can also be bought direct from the grower. As a rule, asparagus is not packaged but sold as an open bundle, tied with raffia. When buying asparagus, this is the only way to be sure that it is really fresh. The surface of the cut ends should not be dry but still moist to the touch; the stems must be firm, smooth and shiny, while the tips should be tight and still closed. Occasionally, growers pack asparagus in a paper tube from which only the

tips show. Here you have to be careful, since this kind of packaging often leads to the development of mould on the stems. It is therefore advisable to check for mould before buying.

The decision to buy white, green or the more rarely available wild asparagus is primarily a question of taste. White asparagus has the most delicate, least pronounced flavour. For this reason, green asparagus is preferred by some, and it is certainly better as an accompaniment to spicy dishes or other strongly-floavoured dishes because of its more intense flavour. Wild asparagus is also green, often even dark green. Its stems are very thin and its flavour is rather different from that of its cultivated relative: it is slightly bitter and not to everyone's taste.

Asparagus must be bought very fresh and consumed as soon as possible. If stored properly fresh asparagus can be kept for two or three days in the refrigerator. Wash the asparagus, dry it thoroughly and cut the ends off so as to create a new cut surface. Now wrap the asparagus in a clean, well moistened – but not wet – tea towel, and put it in the vegetable drawer of the refrigerator. But remember: the longer the asparagus is kept, the less flavour it will have.

Asparagus can also easily be frozen. Peel the asparagus and put them on a flat dish without touching each other. Put this in the freezer. After a few hours the asparagus will be frozen. It can now be divided into the required portions and packed in freezer bags. These can be kept in the freezer for up to three months.

When preparing defrosted asparagus, the cooking time should be reduced by five minutes because it has been frozen.

Tips for cooking asparagus

Whether green or white, asparagus must first be washed thoroughly, especially the tips because they often contain sand. They should therefore be rinsed under running water to remove all traces of sand. White asparagus should always be peeled, while green asparagus should only be peeled when the outside is woody. There are special asparagus peelers on the market, but a potato peeler or a sharp, smooth knife can also be used. Cut a good chunk off the ends because there is nothing more unpleasant than woody asparagus.

If you are cooking large amounts of asparagus, it is worth buying a special asparagus kettle. This makes it

possible to cook the asparagus upright with the tender tips sticking out of the water so that they cook very gently in the hot steam.

When cooking asparagus, use as little water as possible so that it loses the minimum amount of flavour. The addition of salt, a pinch of sugar and a little butter will help the asparagus to remain soft and retain its flavour.

A method which is time-consuming but worthwhile is first to cook the ends and peelings of the asparagus for about 20 minutes. Then cook the asparagus in this stock (broth) – this will help this delicious vegetable preserve its delicate aroma.

Eating and drinking

Asparagus is traditionally accompanied by white wine. Young, fresh, fruity white wines with some acidity, perhaps appropriately bottled in spring, are a perfect accompaniment for most asparagus dishes. Stronger tasting, spicy asparagus dishes may require a full-bodied wine such as a Chardonnay, matured in wood, or if you prefer a sharper wine, a Sauvignon Blanc.

But white wine is not obligatory! You can also serve asparagus with rosé, and with some dishes a Pinot Noir will be perfect.

Refined, noble and healthy

It is true that all vegetables are healthy, but it is particularly true of asparagus. The Phoenicians and Romans, and later the crowned heads of Europe, enjoyed asparagus most of all for its sophisticated taste. But in ancient Greece and China, asparagus was considered a medicinal plant which was much appreciated for its healing and health-promoting properties. Asparagus stimulates the metabolism and therefore, as a spring vegetable, it is ideally suited to cleanse and fortify the body after the long winter months. Today it is know that asparagus has fortifying properties, dietary research and food chemistry having shown that it contains many health promoting components. Thus, asparagus derives its purifying properties from the large amount of roughage and bio-substances it contains, which stimulate the digestive system and kidneys. It also contains large amounts of potassium and other minerals and trace elements such as zinc, calcium, phosphorus, iron and magnesium which all have beneficial effect on the body. Zinc promotes the healing of wounds, nourishes the brain and strengthens connective tissues and blood vessels; calcium and phosphorus strengthen the bones, while iron and magnesium stimulate the formation of blood and as a result prevent muscle cramp.

In addition, asparagus contains many vitamins, especially of the B-group which promotes cell growth and a healthy nervous system, thus ensuring healthy skin and hair. The vitamins C and E in asparagus also protect the cells and help to prevent vascular disorders.

Ideal for diabetics and for slimming diets

Asparagus contains very little carbohydrate and it is therefore a delicacy which can be greatly enjoyed by diabetics. Indeed, there is no need to count bread units, since 400 g/14 oz asparagus only corresponds to 1 bread unit. It is also an ideal vegetable for people wanting to lose weight. Asparagus contains hardly any fat, it has a lot of fibre, and it has diuretic properties. This fulfils all the requirements for successful weight loss – it is very low in fat, it promotes healthy digestion, and it has cleansing and diuretic properties. However, if large quantities of asparagus are eaten, it is important to drink plenty of mineral water to ensure that the kidneys function properly, and that the body does not build up too much uric acid.

Salads and soups

Asparagus can be served hot or cold and combined with many other vegetables as well as a wide range of fresh herbs. The range of delicious salad and soup recipes includes Salad of asparagus tips and mangetouts (snow peas) (page 24), Green asparagus and radicchio salad with Parma ham (page 18), Asparagus salad with new potatoes (page 20), and Asparagus and avocado soup with sorrel (page 34). Asparagus and strawberry salad (see page 18) is a refreshing and unusual dish that is definitely worth trying.

Asparagus and strawberry salad

An unusual combination in which the asparagus and strawberries complement each other's delicate flavours most successfully.

❶ Wash the asparagus, remove the woody ends and cook briefly in boiling water, seasoned with salt, sugar and 5 tablespoons of vinegar. Simmer for 5 minutes over a low heat. Remove the asparagus and rinse in ice cold water to cool them down quickly. Arrange in a flat gratin dish.

❷ Make a marinade with 6 tablespoons of the asparagus water, 1 tablespoon vinegar, oil, salt, pepper and a pinch of sugar. Pour over the asparagus, covering it all with the marinade. Leave to stand.

❸ Clean and wash the strawberries. Purée 40 g/1½ oz strawberries. Cut the remaining ones into quarters and sprinkle with sugar so that the fruit produce a little juice. Mix the strawberry purée and strawberry pieces and add to the asparagus. Stir again.

Serves 4. About 167 kcal per serving

400 g/14 oz green asparagus

salt

sugar

60 ml/2 fl oz (6 tablespoons) strawberry vinegar

60 ml/2 fl oz (6 tablespoons) sunflower oil

freshly ground white pepper

160 g/6 oz fresh strawberries

Green asparagus and radicchio salad with Parma ham

This asparagus salad served with white bread or toast is a small but delicious starter in the Italian style.

❶ Wash the asparagus, remove the woody ends and cut into pieces about 2.5 cm/1 in long. Cook in salted boiling water for about 8 minutes until done.

❷ Clean and wash the radicchio, cut into thin strips and stir into the asparagus.

❸ Mix the cider vinegar, apple juice, pepper, salt and oil together to make a marinade and pour over the salad. Sprinkle with Parmesan shavings and garnish with the Parma ham.

Serves 4. About 153 kcal per serving

400 g/14 oz green asparagus

salt

75 g/3 oz chicory salad

3 tablespoons apple vinegar

3 tablespoons apple juice

freshly ground pepper

1 teaspoon oil

2 tablespoons Parmesan cheese, shaved

4 slices Parma ham

Asparagus salad with new potatoes

1 kg/2¼ lb potatoes

500 g/18 oz green asparagus

salt

1 onion

1 soft-boiled (soft-cooked) egg

2 tablespoons vinegar

2 tablespoons olive oil

freshly ground pepper

1 bunch parsley

Asparagus and new potatoes, the ingredients of this particular salad, complement each most beautifully. This aromatic dish is delicious served with pan-fried meat or fish.

❶ Wash the potatoes and boil in their skins. Wash the asparagus and remove the woody ends. Cut the asparagus in to pieces 2 cm/¾ in long and cook in 250 ml/8 fl oz (1 cup) salted boiling water for about 10 minutes until done. Remove from the water and drain.

❷ Bring the asparagus water back to the boil. Pour 2 or 3 tablespoons of it over the peeled, finely chopped onion in the salad bowl, discarding the rest. Shell the hard-boiled egg, dice it and add to the onion mixture. Mix the vinegar, oil, salt and pepper to make a marinade. Pour into the salad bowl and stir well.

❸ Peel the potatoes and cut into slices; add them still hot to the marinade.

❹ Carefully mix together the washed, finely chopped parsley, asparagus and potatoes.

Serves 4. About 243 kcal per serving

Warm asparagus salad

1 kg/2¼ lb white asparagus

100 ml/3½ oz (scant ½ cup) freshly squeezed orange juice

200 ml/7 fl oz (⅞ cup) meat stock (broth)

60 g/2 oz (4 tablespoons) butter

½ teaspoon sugar

salt

8 tablespoons oil

6 tablespoons white wine vinegar

4 tomatoes

8 leaves of basil

freshly ground pepper

4 slices Parma ham

Basil and Parma ham add an Italian touch to this salad which is delicious served with white bread such as ciabatta.

❶ Peel the asparagus and remove the woody ends. Cut into pieces 5 cm/2 in long and put in a pan with a large surface area. Add the orange juice, stock (broth), butter and sugar. Season with salt. Bring quickly to the boil and simmer over a low heat for 10 minutes.

❷ Mix the oil and vinegar and add to the asparagus. Cut the tomatoes into eight and the basil into strips. Add to the asparagus and season with pepper.

❸ Garnish each plate with a slice of Parma ham.

Serves 4. About 296 kcal per serving

Asparagus salad with artichoke hearts

500 g/18 oz white asparagus

salt

1 pinch sugar

10 g/⅜ oz (2 teaspoons) butter

6 small artichoke hearts

4 firm tomatoes

4 shallots

4 tablespoons lemon juice

5 tablespoons olive oil

½ bunch chives

freshly ground pepper

Artichokes or globe artichokes have very large flower heads. These are cut off the plant before they are mature, and the leaves and hairy central core are removed. The part which is eaten is the fleshy heart which remains.

❶ Peel the asparagus, remove the woody ends and cook in boiling water to which sugar and butter have been° added for about 20 minutes until done. Take out of the water, drain and cut into pieces 4 cm/1½ in long.

❷ Drain the artichoke hearts thoroughly and cut in quarters. Wash the tomatoes, remove the stalks (stems) and cut into eight. Wash and prepare the shallots and cut into rings. Add all these ingredients to the asparagus and stir well.

❸ Mix the oil and lemon juice together and stir to make a smooth mixture. Season with salt and add to the salad. Sprinkle with finely chopped chives and pepper.

Serves 4. About 188 kcal per serving

Tofu (bean curd) salad with asparagus

Tofu (bean curd), soy sauce and ginger are very popular ingredients in Oriental cuisine and their light, spicy aroma complements the delicate taste of the asparagus.

❶ Wash the asparagus, remove the woody ends. Cut off the asparagus tips and keep them separate. Cut the rest into pieces 5 cm/2 in long. Bring water to the boil with 1 tablespoon of soya sauce and cook the asparagus tips for 3 minutes. Remove from the water, drain and put to one side. Add the rest of the pieces to the water and cook for 5 minutes, then drain.

❷ To make the salad dressing: mix 4 tablespoons soy sauce, lemon juice, grated lemon zest, sugar and sunflower oil and stir well.

❸ Cut the tofu (bean curd) into cubes. Wash and trim the spring onion (scallion). Peel the red onion. Cut both into rings. Pull the leaves off the watercress. Mix all the ingredients with the asparagus pieces, stirring very carefully.

❹ Peel the ginger, grate finely and sprinkle over the salad. Garnish with the asparagus tips.

Serves 4. About 215 kcal per serving

450 g/1 lb green asparagus

5 tablespoons soy sauce

juice and zest of ½ untreated lemon

3 teaspoons sugar

5 tablespoons sunflower oil

300 g/11 oz tofu (bean curd)

1 spring onion (scallion)

1 red onion

30 g/1 oz watercress

piece of fresh ginger, about 3 cm/1¼ in long

Asparagus salad with a vinaigrette dressing

1 kg/2¼ lb green asparagus

1 tablespoon lemon juice

1 pinch sugar

1 pinch salt

4 eggs

yolks of 2 eggs

2 tablespoons olive oil

1 tablespoon wine vinegar

1½ teaspoon Dijon mustard

2 teaspoons capers

4 tablespoons red wine

freshly ground pepper

salt

30 g/1 oz parsley

chervil to taste

A vinaigrette prepared with eggs, capers and red wine, turns this quick, easy asparagus salad into a delicious, sophisticated dish.

❶ Wash the asparagus, remove the woody ends and simmer in gently boiling water seasoned with lemon juice, sugar and salt for about 10 minutes. Remove the asparagus from the water and leave to cool.

❷ Hard-boil (hard-cook) the eggs, shell and separate the yolks from the whites. Chop the egg whites finely and put to one side. Crush the egg yolks with a fork, add to the 2 raw egg yolks and stir in the olive oil, vinegar, mustard, capers and red wine. Season with salt and pepper.

❸ Wash the parsley and the chervil and wipe dry. Chop finely and stir into the vinaigrette together with the chopped egg white.

❹ Arrange the asparagus on a dish and pour the vinaigrette over them.

Serves 4. About 218 kcal per serving

Salad of asparagus tips and mangetouts (snow peas)

500 g/18 oz green asparagus tips

400 g/14 oz mangetouts (snow peas)

250 g/9 oz coloured salad leaves

5 tablespoons olive oil

1 tablespoon balsamic vinegar

salt

freshly ground pepper

80 g/3 oz Parmesan, shaved

watercress for garnish

Mangetouts (snow peas) are a vegetable as delicate as asparagus. Both require very little cooking.

❶ Wash the asparagus tips and cut once lengthways. Wash and prepare the mangetouts (snow peas) and cook together with the asparagus in a small amount of gently boiling water until done.

❷ Wash the salad leaves and arrange on four plates; place the asparagus tips and mangetouts (snow peas) on top. Mix the olive oil, balsamic vinegar, salt and pepper and sprinkle over the salad, asparagus and mangetouts (snow peas).

❸ Slice shavings of Parmesan and sprinkle on the salad, asparagus and mangetouts (snow peas). Garnish with watercress.

Serves 4. About 295 kcal per serving

Creamed asparagus soup with watercress

Excellent asparagus stock (broth) is made by boiling the woody asparagus ends and peelings. The more concentrated the stock (broth), the more delicious and fragrant the soup will be.

❶ Peel the asparagus and remove the woody ends. Boil the woody asparagus ends and peelings in 1.5 litres/2¾ pints (7 cups) salted water for about 30 minutes until the liquid has reduced by almost one-third. Strain this stock (broth) through a sieve into a second saucepan.

❷ Cut the asparagus tips into pieces about 2.5 cm/1in long and cook in the gently simmering asparagus stock (broth) for about 5–7 minutes until done. Remove from the stock (broth) and drain. Cut the asparagus pieces into thin slices.

❸ Peel the onion and chop finely. Put 1 tablespoon of the melted butter in a saucepan and add the finely chopped onion. Braise lightly until transparent. Add 250 ml/8 fl oz (1 cup) asparagus stock (broth). Add the asparagus slices, sugar and stock (bouillon) cube and simmer over a low heat for about 20 minutes.

❹ Purée the asparagus and slowly pour 250 ml/8 fl oz (1 cup) asparagus stock (broth) into the soup while stirring. Strain the soup through a sieve, purée again and add the cream. Dilute the cornflour (cornstarch) in a little water and stir into the soup with a whisk. Bring to the boil. Add ice-cold butter and whisk until foamy. Season with salt, pepper and nutmeg. Add the asparagus tips, heat up again and garnish with the watercress.

Serves 4. About 248 kcal per serving

1 kg/2¼ lb white asparagus

salt

1 onion

25 g/1 oz (2 tablespoons) butter

1 tablespoon sugar

½ stock (bouillon) cube

250 ml/8 fl oz (1 cup) cream

1 teaspoon cornflour (cornstarch)

freshly ground white pepper

freshly grated nutmeg

watercress as garnish

Creamy asparagus soup

This classic recipe has an irresistible, delicate asparagus flavour.

1 kg/2¼ lb white asparagus

salt

1 teaspoon sugar

100 g/3½ oz (½ cup) butter

60 g/2¼ oz (¾ cup) flour

250 ml/8 fl oz (1 cup) cream

2 egg yolks

freshly ground pepper

juice and zest of 1 untreated lemon

1 bunch chives

❶ Wash the asparagus thoroughly and cut off the woody ends. Add the woody asparagus ends and peelings to 1.5 litres/2¾ pints (7 cups) boiling water with a pinch of sugar and simmer over a moderate heat for about 15 minutes. Strain the asparagus stock (broth) through a sieve into a second saucepan. Add the asparagus pieces to this stock (broth) and cook for 15-20 minutes until done.

❷ Melt the butter in a saucepan, stir in the flour, and slowly add the asparagus stirring all the time. Simmer gently for about 15 minutes.

❸ Mix the cream and egg yolk together and stir into the soup. Heat again but do not bring to the boil.

❹ Add the asparagus pieces to the soup. Season with salt, pepper and the juice and zest of a lemon. Garnish with finely chopped chives.

Serves 4. About 493 kcal per serving

Asparagus and cheese soup

The baguette and pastis give this asparagus soup a distinctive southern French touch. A glass of pastis would be the perfect aperitif.

300 g/11 oz green asparagus

300 g/11 oz white asparagus

salt

150 g/5½ oz processed cheese

½ teaspoon paprika pepper

4 baguette slices

sugar

freshly ground white pepper

3 tablespoons Pastis

❶ Wash the green asparagus, peel the white asparagus and remove the woody ends. Cook the woody ends and peelings in 500 ml/17 fl oz (2¼ cups) boiling water for 30 minutes. Strain the asparagus stock (broth) through a sieve into a second saucepan.

❷ Cut the asparagus into pieces about 2.5 cm/1 in long and cook in the reduced asparagus stock (broth) for 15 minutes.

❸ Mix together the soft processed cheese and paprika and spread on the baguette slices. Toast under the grill for 2 minutes until golden yellow.

❹ Season the asparagus with salt, pepper, sugar and pastis. Pour into four soup bowls and garnish with the toasted cheese baguette slices.

Serves 4. About 198 kcal per serving

Italian asparagus soup

This Italian recipe is served with croutons or, to use the Italian word, crostini.

❶ Wash the asparagus, cut off the woody ends and remove the tips.

❷ Heat the oil and butter in a large saucepan. Add the finely chopped onions and braise gently until golden yellow. Add the cut asparagus and cook for a few minutes. Season with salt, add the vegetable stock (broth) and simmer over a low heat for about 1 hour.

❸ Strain the asparagus stock (broth) through a sieve into a second saucepan. Rub the asparagus through the sieve, add to the stock (broth) and stir well. Add the asparagus tips. Simmer for another 5 minutes.

❹ Sprinkle the soup with finely chopped parsley. Serve with Parmesan and croutons.

Serves 4. About 339 kcal per serving

500 g/18 oz green asparagus

20 g/¾ oz (1½ tablespoons) butter

20 ml/1 fl oz (2 tablespoons) olive oil

3 onions

salt

2 litres/3½ pints (9 cups) vegetable stock (broth)

1 bunch parsley

100 g/3½ oz (1 cup) finely grated Parmesan

croutons

Asparagus soup with omelette

An exquisite, traditional recipe which has given great pleasure to many people over the years.

❶ Wash the asparagus and remove the woody ends. Cut into small pieces and simmer gently in salted water with a pinch of sugar for about 10 minutes. Wash the parsley, wipe dry and chop finely.

❷ Melt the butter in a large saucepan, add the asparagus and half the parsley. Sprinkle with flour and cook gently. Add the meat stock (broth) and simmer over a low heat.

❸ Mix together the eggs, egg yolks, cream and flour, season with salt and pepper. Cook the omelette until it is quite firm. Remove from the pan and cut into fine strips. Stir gently into the soup and season with nutmeg. Garnish with parsley.

Serves 4. About 450 kcal per serving

1.5 kg/3 lb green asparagus

salt

1 pinch sugar

1 bunch parsley

60 g/2 oz (4 tablespoons) butter

1 tablespoon flour

1.5 litres/2¾ pints (7 cups) meat stock (broth)

finely grated nutmeg

For the omelette:

2 eggs

yolks of 2 egg

125 ml/4 fl oz (½ cup) cream

3 tablespoons flour

salt

freshly ground pepper

Green asparagus soup with salmon trout

1 kg/2¼ lb green asparagus

salt

1 pinch sugar

2 sprigs tarragon

1 onion

25 g/1 oz (2 tablespoons) clarified butter

1 large potato

4 tablespoons cream

freshly ground white pepper

150 g/5½ oz smoked salmon trout

Green asparagus has a stronger taste than white asparagus. In this recipe it is perfectly complemented by the tarragon and salmon trout.

❶ Wash the asparagus thoroughly and remove the woody ends. Cook the woody ends in 1 litre/1¾ pints (4½ cups) salted water, flavoured with a pinch of sugar and 1 sprig of tarragon for 15 minutes.

❷ Peel the onion, chop finely and braise lightly in clarified butter until golden yellow. Dice the peeled potatoes, add to the saucepan and season with a little salt. Add some water, cover and cook.

❸ Strain the asparagus stock (broth) through a sieve into a second saucepan. Cut the asparagus into pieces 3 cm/1¼ in long, add the strained stock (broth) and cook for 10 minutes. Remove from the stock (broth) and drain. Remove the asparagus tips from the rest of the asparagus. Add half the remaining asparagus pieces to the saucepan with the onion and potatoes. Stir in ¾ of the asparagus stock (broth). Add the cream and stir. Add the rest of the asparagus and the remaining tarragon leaves. Season with salt and pepper.

❹ Cut the salmon trout into small pieces and add to the soup.

Serves 4. About 177 kcal per serving

Asparagus soup with coconut

This Oriental soup with its distinctive taste of coconut and lemon adds a festive note to any meal. Instead of fish fillets you can also use chicken breasts. The ingredients needed to make this soup are available in most oriental food shops.

300 g/11 oz green asparagus

50 g/2 oz mangetouts (snow peas)

50 g/2 oz peas

4 spring onions (scallions)

1 leek

1 red peppper

300 g/11 oz white fish fillets

juice and peel of ½ untreated lemon

salt

1 pinch sugar

800 ml/1¾ pints (3½ cups) coconut milk

100 ml/3½ oz (scant ½ cup) medium white wine

15 leaves lemon balm

❶ Wash the asparagus, remove the woody ends and cut into pieces 2 cm/¾ in long. Wash and prepare the mangetouts (snow peas), peas, spring onions (scallions) and leek. Chop the mangetouts (snow peas) and cut the spring onions and leek into rings.

❷ Cut the red pepper into two. Remove the stalk, seeds and white fleshy skin inside. Wash and cut into very fine slices.

❸ Rinse the fish fillets in cold water, wipe dry and sprinkle with lemon juice.

❹ Bring 250 ml/8 fl oz (1 cup) water to the boil, seasoned with salt and sugar; add the asparagus and cook for 5 minutes. Add the coconut milk and wine, 5 leaves of lemon balm and the vegetables. Cook for another 5 minutes. Put the fish in the soup and leave to stand for 5 minutes. Add the red pepper and season the soup.

❺ Wash the remaining lemon balm, wipe dry and sprinkle on the soup when it has cooled down slightly.

Serves 4. About 146 kcal per serving

Creamed white and green asparagus soup

Naturally this soup can also be prepared with just one kind of asparagus. White asparagus has a very delicate flavour while green asparagus has a stronger taste.

250 g/9 oz green asparagus

250 g/9 oz white asparagus

salt

1 pinch sugar

50 g/2 oz (4 tablespoons) butter

30 g/1 oz (good ½ cup) flour

125 ml/4 fl oz (½ cup) cream

yolks of 2 eggs

freshly ground white pepper

juice and zest of ½ untreated
    lemon

chives as garnish

❶ Wash the green asparagus thoroughly, peel the white asparagus and remove the woody ends. Add the woody ends and peelings to 1 litre/1¾ pints (4½ cups) salted water with a pinch of sugar, and bring to the boil. Cover and simmer gently for 15 minutes. Strain the stock (broth) into a second saucepan.

❷ Cut the asparagus into small pieces. Cook the white asparagus for about 12 minutes and the green asparagus for about 8 minutes in the stock (broth) until done. Remove from the asparagus stock (broth) and drain.

❸ Prepare the roux and gradually add the asparagus stock (broth) to it, stirring all the time. Leave to stand for 15 minutes. Mix together the cream and egg yolks, add 3 tablespoons asparagus and stir. Add this mixture to the soup. Heat up again but do not bring to the boil. Season with salt, pepper, lemon juice and grated lemon zest.

❹ Now add the asparagus pieces to the soup and garnish with the finely chopped chives.

Serves 4. About 266 kcal per serving

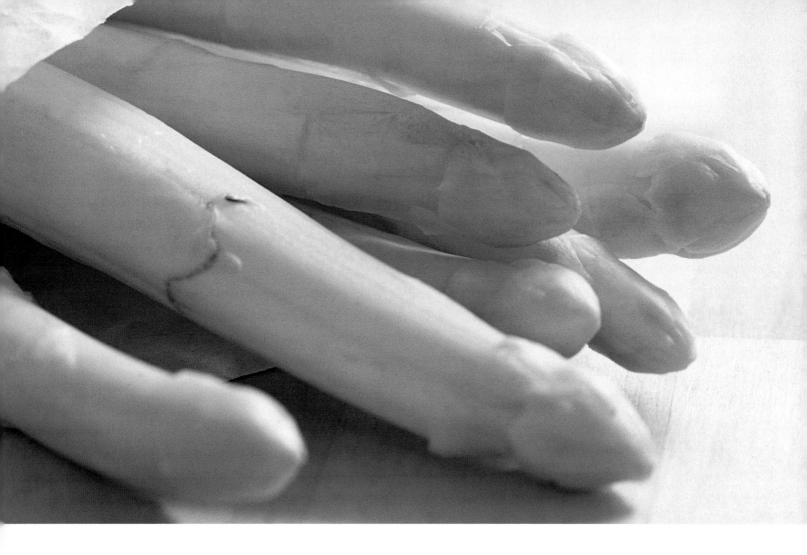

Asparagus and avocado soup with sorrel

Sorrel has a powerful, slightly bitter taste. With delicately flavoured vegetables such as asparagus and avocado, it should be used sparingly.

700 g/1½ lb white asparagus

700 ml/1½ pints (3 cups) vegetable stock (broth)

1 avocado

4 tablespoons sour cream

2 tablespoons lemon juice

salt

freshly ground pepper

some finely chopped sorrel

❶ Peel the asparagus, remove the woody ends, cut about 4 cm/1¼ in off the tips and chop up the rest of the asparagus. Cook the asparagus tips in the vegetable stock (broth) for about 5 minutes until done. Remove from the stock (broth) and strain.

❷ Now add the remaining chopped asparagus to the vegetable stock (broth) and simmer gently. Purée and press through a conical sieve.

❸ Halve the avocado, remove the stone (seed), peel and chop up. Purée with a little asparagus stock (broth), add to the soup and bring to the boil. Add the lemon juice and sour cream. Season with salt and pepper.

❹ Add the asparagus tips and sorrel to the soup.

Serves 4. About 183 kcal per serving

Iced asparagus soup

Asparagus soup is also very delicious cold. It is most refreshing on a warm summer's day during the asparagus season.

❶ Wash the asparagus and remove the woody ends. Cut the tips off half the asparagus. Reserve the tips. Cut the rest of the asparagus into small pieces.

❷ Peel the onion, shallot and clove of garlic, chop finely and braise lightly in hot butter until golden yellow. Stir in the asparagus, add 1 litre/1¾ pints (4½ cups) boiling water and simmer over a low heat for 30 minutes.

❸ Purée the asparagus, bring back to the boil, stir in the crème fraîche and simmer gently until the soup has thickened a little. Season with salt, pepper and nutmeg; remove from the heat and leave to cool down. Then put in the refrigerator for at least 6 hours.

❹ Cook the asparagus tips for 2 minutes in salted boiling water. Pour away the water and drain. Leave to cool.

❺ Pour the iced soup into four soup bowls, add the cold asparagus tips and sprinkle with finely chopped parsley.

Serves 4. About 162 kcal per serving

1 kg/2¼ lb green asparagus
1 large onion
1 shallot
1 clove garlic
40 g/1½ oz (3 tablespoons) butter
3 tablespoons crème fraîche
salt
freshly ground pepper
freshly grated nutmeg
½ bunch parsley

Light dishes

Rice and pasta are ideal accompaniments to light asparagus dishes, such as Tagliatelle with green asparagus and chanterelles (page 38), Asparagus ravioli (see page 40) or Asparagus risotto (page 48), which are all inspired by Italian cooking. On the other hand, French cuisine is the inspiration behind Salmon crêpes with asparagus (page 47) and Asparagus crêpes with curd cheese (page 50). Here there are also some classic German asparagus dishes, such as Asparagus pieces in chervil sauce (page 53) or Asparagus with ham and potatoes (page 45). A slightly spicy alternative to the usually mild asparagus recipes is Asparagus omelette (page 44).

Tagliatelle with green asparagus and chanterelles

The warm colours of this delicious pasta and asparagus dish make it a pleasure to the eye as well as the palate.

1 kg/2¼ lb green asparagus

salt

50 g/2 oz (4 tablespoons) butter

250 g/9 oz tagliatelle

4 slices smoked ham

250 g/9 oz fresh chanterelles

1 shallot

1 sprig thyme

6 tablespoons olive oil

freshly ground pepper

125 g/4½ oz (1¼ cups) freshly grated or shaved Parmesan cheese

❶ Wash the asparagus, remove the woody ends, halve lengthways and cook gently in boiling water for about 5 minutes until cooked. Remove from the water, drain and keep warm in a pan on the stove with about 20 g/¾ oz (1½ tablespoons) butter.

❷ Cook the tagliatelle *al dente* in the asparagus stock (broth). Cut the ham into strips.

❸ Clean and wash the chanterelles, peel and chop the shallot. Remove the leaves from the sprig of thyme and braise the chanterelles, shallots and thyme lightly in the remaining butter for about 5–8 minutes.

❹ Drain the tagliatelle and arrange in plates together with the asparagus and chanterelles. Put the ham on top and sprinkle with olive oil. Season with salt and pepper and sprinkle with Parmesan.

Serves 4. About 650 kcal per serving

Carpaccio with raw asparagus

For this dish it is particularly important that the asparagus should be very fresh and tender because it will not be cooked but only slightly marinated.

8 sticks green asparagus

2 tablespoons lemon juice

salt

freshly ground pepper

5 tablespoons sunflower oil

60 g/2 oz Parma or similar dried ham

1 bunch rocket

❶ Wash the asparagus and remove the woody ends. Cut the asparagus diagonally into slices 2 mm/⅒ in thick.

❷ Mix the lemon juice, salt, pepper and oil to make a marinade. Pour over the asparagus, stir gently and leave to stand for a while.

❸ Arrange the ham on four plates and put the marinated asparagus on top. Wash the rocket and dry. Put on top of the asparagus and sprinkle with pepper.

Serves 4. About 119 kcal per serving

Asparagus ravioli

Ravioli with meat filling are available from supermarkets and Italian delicatessen. They can be either frozen or fresh.

1.5 kg/3 lb white asparagus

salt

1 pinch sugar

10 g/⅜ oz (2 teaspoons) butter

600 g/1¼ lb fresh ravioli with meat filling

1 shallot

6 tablespoons white wine-vinegar

freshly ground pepper

4 tablespoons broth

yolks of 2 eggs

2 tablespoons olive oil

2 tablespoons tarragon, finely chopped

3 tablespoons chopped tomatoes

cayenne pepper

❶ Peel the asparagus and remove the woody ends. Cook in boiling salted water with sugar and butter until done.

❷ Cook the ravioli *al dente* in gently simmering water.

❸ Peel the shallots, dice and cook with the vinegar and pepper. Reduce to thicken the mixture. Add the stock (broth).

❹ Add 2 tablespoons water to the egg yolk and beat in a bain-marie until it becomes creamy. Add the shallot mixture, stir in the oil, add the tarragon and tomatoes and mix all the ingredients together. Season with salt and cayenne pepper. Heat carefully but do not bring to the boil.

❺ Put the ravioli and asparagus in a large bowl or arrange on large plates and pour the sauce on top.

Serves 4. About 462 kcal per serving

Green asparagus with Parmesan shavings

Thin shavings can be sliced from mature, hard Parmesan with a mandoline or cucumber slicer.

4 slices Parma ham

1 kg/2¼ lb green asparagus

salt

2 tablespoons olive oil

1 teaspoon vinegar

freshly ground pepper

60 g/2 oz Parmesan cheese, shaved

❶ Fry the Parma ham until crisp. Remove from the pan, leave to cool and cut into strips.

❷ Wash the asparagus and remove the woody ends. Cook in salted water for about 10 minutes until done. Remove from the water, drain and arrange on plates.

❸ Mix the olive oil, vinegar, salt and pepper to make the dressing. Stir well and pour over the asparagus. Garnish with the Parma ham and Parmesan shavings.

Serves 4. About 205 kcal per serving

Tagliatelle with asparagus and broccoli

250 g/9 oz white asparagus

400 g/14 oz broccoli

2 cloves garlic

50 g/2 oz (4 tablespoons) butter

salt

freshly ground pepper

250 g/9 oz mascarpone

250 g/9 oz tagliatelle

Tagliatelle is made in various colours. The creamy-coloured kind is best to combine with asparagus and broccoli.

❶ Peel the asparagus, remove the woody ends and cut into pieces 2 cm/¾ in long. Clean and wash the broccoli and separate the florets. Peel the cloves of garlic and chop finely. Add to the broccoli and asparagus and braise lightly in the butter. Cover and cook over a low heat for 4 minutes. Season with salt and butter. Add the mascarpone, stir well and cook until the sauce becomes creamy.

❷ Cook the tagliatelle *al dente* in 2–3 litres/3½–5 pints (9–13 cups) of boiling water. Pour away the water and drain. Arrange the tagliatelle on plates and garnish with the vegetables.

Serves 4. About 609 kcal per serving

Asparagus risotto with Serrano ham

1 kg/2¼ lb green asparagus

salt

2 onions

2 clove garlic

2 tablespoons olive oil

200 g/7 oz (1 xup) risotto rice

750 ml/1¼ pints (3¼ cups) vegetable stock (broth)

4 tablespoons grated Manchego or Parmesan cheese

4 tablespoons chopped basil

freshly ground pepper

100 g/3½ oz Serrano ham, thinly sliced

Instead of Manchego cheese, which is not available everywhere, this herb risotto can also be made with mature Parmesan.

❶ Wash the asparagus and remove the woody ends. Cut into pieces 2 cm/1¼ in long and cook in gently simmering salted water for about 12 minutes. Remove from the water and drain.

❷ Peel the onions and garlic, chop finely and fry in hot oil until golden yellow. Add the rice, fry lightly, add the stock (broth) gradually while stirring until the rice has softened. This will take about 20 minutes.

❸ Stir the asparagus into the risotto, add the cheese and basil. Season with salt and pepper. Put in a bowl and garnish with ham.

Serves 4. About 437 kcal per serving

Veal olives stuffed with asparagus

Veal olives stuffed with asparagus make a delicious combination.

600 g/1¼ lb green asparagus

salt

1 pinch sugar

1 teaspoon butter

4 thin veal escalopes

4 slices uncooked ham

6 tablespoons oil

50 ml/1½ fl oz (5 tablespoons) dry, medium white wine

400 ml/14 fl oz (1¾ cups) meat stock (broth)

1 small onion

½ bunch parsley

2 tablespoons balsamic vinegar

freshly ground pepper

some flour

❶ Wash the asparagus and remove the woody ends. Blanch for about 3 minutes in salted water together with a pinch of salt and butter. Remove from the water and drain.

❷ Rinse the veal escalopes under the tap, wipe dry and put a slice of ham on top of each one. For each veal olive, cut four pieces of asparagus in half and wrap in a veal escalope. Secure with skewers. Fry the veal olives on all sides in 1 tablespoon hot oil. Add the white wine and beef stock (broth). Cover and cook for 30 minutes.

❸ Mix the finely chopped onion and parsley with 5 tablespoons oil and balsamic vinegar. Season with salt and pepper. Cut the remaining asparagus into pieces 3 cm/1¼ in long and stir into the vinaigrette.

❸ Remove the veal olives from the sauce. Season the sauce with salt and pepper and thicken with a little flour if desired. Remove the skewers and slice the veal olives diagonally. Arrange on plates with the sauce and asparagus salad.

Serves 4. About 441 kcal per serving

Asparagus omelette

A delicious omelette variation containing a tasty surprise for your guests.

600 g/1¼ lb white asparagus

600 g/1¼ lb green asparagus

salt

1 pinch sugar

1 teaspoon butter

1 shallot

1 gherkin

25 g/1 oz mixed herbs

150 g/5½ oz yoghurt

5 tablespoons oil

1 teaspoon mustard

cayenne pepper

6 eggs

2 tablespoons milk

1 tablespoon chives

freshly ground pepper

a few chervil leaves

❶ Peel the white asparagus, wash the green asparagus, remove the woody ends. Cook the asparagus for about 20 minutes in gently simmering salted watering together with sugar and butter.

❷ Peel the shallot and chop coarsely. Chop up the gherkin. Purée the chopped shallot and gherkin with the mixed herbs, yoghurt and 1 tablespoon of oil. Season with salt, mustard and cayenne pepper.

❸ Separate the eggs. Mix the egg yolks, chives and pepper and fold in the stiffly beaten egg whites. Make four omelettes, one after the other.

❹ Remove the asparagus from the water, drain and arrange on one half of the omelette. Fold the other half over the asparagus. Pour the herb sauce over the omelette and garnish with chervil leaves.

Serves 4. About 326 kcal per serving

Asparagus with ham and potatoes

White asparagus with ham and new potatoes with melted butter is a real classic among asparagus dishes. Instead of a single kind of ham, you could also use a combination of smoked, cooked and Parma ham.

❶ Wash the asparagus, peel and remove the woody ends. Boil the woody ends and peelings in 2.5 litres/4½ pints (11 cups) salted water for about 30 minutes until the liquid has reduced by one-third. Pour the reduced stock (broth) into a second saucepan, add 1 tablespoon butter and the sugar and bring to the boil again. Cook the asparagus in this stock (broth) over a medium heat for 15–20 minutes.

❷ Wash the potatoes, boil and drain.

❸ Wash the tomatoes and basil and wipe dry. Arrange the ham on a dish and garnish with the cherry tomatoes and basil.

❹ Wash the parsley, wipe dry and chop finely. Melt the remaining butter. Remove the skin from the potatoes, put in a bowl and garnish with about half the parsley. Remove the asparagus from the water, drain and arrange on a dish. Pour 4 tablespoons of melted butter over all and sprinkle with parsley. Serve the melted butter in sauce boat.

Serves 4. About 1044 kcal per serving

2 kg/4½ lb white asparagus

salt

2 teaspoons sugar

250 g/9 oz (1 cup) butter

1 kg/2¼ lb potatoes

4 cherry tomatoes

a few leaves of basil

600 g/1¼ lb cooked ham, thinly sliced

½ bunch parsley

Egg fricassée with asparagus

In this particular dish, the asparagus is merely part of the sauce. Nevertheless, it gives this fricassée a very special touch.

500 g/18 oz green asparagus

salt

1 pinch sugar

8 eggs

250 ml/8 fl oz (1 cup) milk

250 ml/8 fl oz (1 cup) cream

50 g/2 oz (4 tablespoons) butter

80 g/3 oz porridge (rolled) oats

freshly ground pepper

juice of ½ lemon

1 bunch parsley

❶ Wash the asparagus thoroughly, removing the woody ends. Cut the asparagus into pieces 3 cm/1¼ in long and cook in salted water with a pinch of sugar for about 10 minutes until done. Remove from the water and drain.

❷ Hard-boil (hard-cook) the eggs, shell and cut in slices with an egg-slicer.

❸ Mix 250 ml/8 fl oz (1 cup) asparagus stock (broth), milk and cream and bring to the boil together with the butter. Stir the Porridge (rolled) oats into a small amount of asparagus stock (broth), add to the milk and cream mixture, and bring back to the boil.

❹ Add the asparagus and eggs to the sauce and heat up slowly over a low heat. Leave to infuse. Season with salt, pepper and lemon juice and garnish with finely chopped parsley.

Serves 4. About 569 kcal per serving

Asparagus flan

This exquisite asparagus flan with watercress can also be made in individual portions. It is delicious served with a herb sauce and white bread.

500 g/18 oz white asparagus

500 g/18 oz green asparagus

500 ml/16 fl oz (2 cups) cream

6 eggs

salt

freshly ground pepper

zest of 1 untreated lemon

butter to grease the mould

watercress as garnish

❶ Peel the white asparagus, wash the green asparagus, remove the woody ends and cut the asparagus stalks (stems) into slices 1 cm/⅜ in thick.

❷ Whisk the cream and eggs into a creamy mixture. Season with salt, pepper and lemon zest. Stir in the asparagus. Grease a gratin dish and its lid generously. Pour the asparagus mixture into the gratin dish up to 4 cm/1½ in below the edge. Cover and cook in the hot bain-marie for 50 minutes.

❸ Remove the gratin dish from the bain-marie, allow to rest for 5 minutes. Turn upside down onto a large serving dish and garnish with the previously washed watercress.

Serves 4. About 514 kcal per serving

Salmon crêpes with asparagus

Crêpes, the very thin French pancakes, might almost have been invented to enhance the delicate flavour of salmon and asparagus.

❶ Quickly work the flour, milk, eggs and melted butter to a smooth mixture. Season with salt and nutmeg. Add finely chopped chives and leave the batter to stand for a while.

❷ Wash the green asparagus, peel the white asparagus and remove the woody ends. Cook the asparagus in salted water with 1 pinch of sugar and 1 teaspoon butter for about 15 minutes. Remove the asparagus from the water, drain and keep in a warm place.

❸ Stir the hollandaise sauce mix in 125 ml/4 fl oz (1 cup) cold water and bring slowly to the boil, stirring constantly. Add the remaining butter and stir constantly over a low heat until the butter has completely melted.

❹ Heat the oil in a pan and make very thin golden-brown crêpes with the batter. Stuff the crêpes with a slice of salmon and asparagus. Arrange on individual plates and pour the hollandaise sauce over the crêpes.

Serves 4. About 663 kcal per serving

For the pastry:
80 g/3 oz (generous ¾ cup) flour
200 ml/7 fl oz (⅞ cup) milk
2 eggs
25 g/1 oz (2 tablespoons) butter
salt
freshly grated nutmeg
1 bunch chives

Other ingredients:
750 g/1½ lb green asparagus
750 g/1½ lb white asparagus
salt
1 pinch sugar
125 g/4½ oz (⅝ cup) butter
1 packet hollandaise sauce mix
4 tablespoons oil
200 g/7 oz smoked salmon

Asparagus risotto

6 sticks green asparagus

6 sticks white asparagus

salt

1 teaspoon butter

1 pinch sugar

2 tablespoons cream

1 onion

2 tablespoons oil

200 g/7 oz (1 cup) risotto rice

100 ml/3½ oz (scant ½ cup) dry
  white wine

freshly ground white pepper

100 g/3½ oz (1 cup) grated
  Parmesan

chives for garnish

A good risotto requires patience. You can only add a small of water at a time and then you have to wait until it has been completely absorbed until adding more.

❶ Wash the green asparagus, peel the white asparagus and remove the woody ends. Cook the white asparagus for 15 minutes and the green asparagus for 10 minutes in salted water with butter and a pinch of sugar. Remove from the water and drain. Cut the tips off the asparagus, and cut the rest of the stalks (stems) into pieces 1 cm/⅜ in long. Purée one-third of the asparagus pieces with cream.

❷ Chop the onion finely, braise in the hot oil, add the rice and fry until golden yellow. Mix 750 ml/1¼ pints (3¼ cups) asparagus stock (broth) with the white wine. Pour onto the rice little by little, stirring constantly, until all the liquid has been absorbed. Season the risotto with salt and pepper, stir in the asparagus purée and asparagus pieces, add the Parmesan and stir well. Garnish with chives.

Serves 4. About 360 kcal per serving

Asparagus with saffron and almond hollandaise sauce

1 kg/2¼ lb green asparagus

1 kg/2¼ lb white asparagus

salt

1 pinch sugar

10 g/⅜ oz (2 teaspoons) butter

For the hollandaise sauce:

1 pinch threads of saffron

2 teaspoons lemon juice

salt

freshly ground pepper

3 egg yolks

200 g/7 oz (1 cup) butter

25 g/1 oz (¼ cup) flaked (slivered) almonds

Saffron is a very interesting spice, consisting of the dried pigments of the autumn crocus.

❶ Wash the green asparagus, peel the white asparagus and remove the woody ends. Cook the white asparagus for about 10 minutes and the green asparagus for about 8 minutes in gently simmering salted water together with sugar and butter.

❷ To make the hollandaise sauce: dissolve the saffron in 4 teaspoons hot water, add the lemon juice, salt, pepper and egg yolk and stir until the mixture is smooth. Whisk over a bain-marie until foamy. Gradually add the lumps of butter and finally the lightly roasted almonds.

❸ Remove the asparagus from the stock (broth), drain and serve with the hollandaise sauce.

Serves 4. About 553 kcal per serving

Asparagus crêpes with curd cheese

For the filling:

750 g/1½ lb white asparagus

salt

450 g/1 lb curd cheese

zest of 1 untreated lemon

freshly ground pepper

For the pastry:

100 g/3½ oz (1 cup) flour

½ teaspoon salt

2 eggs

1 teaspoon olive oil

125 ml/4 fl oz (½ cup) milk

300 ml/10 fl oz (1¼ cups) coffee cream

The curd cheese and coffee cream give this asparagus dish a delicious creamy note.

❶ Peel the asparagus and remove the woody ends. Cook the asparagus in gently simmering salted water until done. Remove from the water, drain and cut into pieces 2 cm/1¼ in long.

❷ Mix the curd cheese with the grated lemon zest, stir in the asparagus and season with salt and pepper.

❸ Mix the flour, salt, eggs, oil, milk and 125 ml/4 fl oz (½ cup) of water and work into a smooth batter. Make 12 thin crêpes.

❹ Place some of the asparagus-curd mixture on each crêpe, and roll it up. Put the crêpes in a large, flat gratin dish. Pour the coffee cream over the crêpes, cover with aluminium foil and bake in the oven preheated to 180°C (350°F), Gas mark 4 for 20–30 minutes.

Serves 4. About 867 kcal per serving

Asparagus with fresh morels

Whether pointed or round, morels are a luxury which add a further touch of refinement to this asparagus dish.

20 small potatoes, parboiled

1 tablespoon groundnut oil

60 g/2 oz (4½ tablespoons) butter

salt

1 kg/2¼ lb white asparagus

150 g/5½ oz fresh morels

freshly ground pepper

4 tablespoons cream

freshly grated nutmeg

4 tablespoons chicken stock (broth)

1 tablespoon smooth parsley

❶ Wash the potatoes, cook in their skins, peel and brown lightly in groundnut oil and ½ tablespoon butter. Season with salt.

❷ Peel the asparagus and remove the woody ends. Cook in gently simmering salted water. Remove the asparagus from the water, cool quickly in ice-cold water and drain. Heat up again slowly in a casserole with 2 tablespoons butter and keep warm.

❸ Prepare and wash the morels. Brown lightly in 2 tablespoons butter. Season with salt and butter.

❹ Season the cream with salt, pepper and nutmeg and reduce to thicken. Season the poultry stock (broth) with salt and pepper and reduce.

❺ Arrange the asparagus, potatoes and morels on a large serving dish. Pour the cream sauce, chicken stock (broth) and asparagus butter on top and garnish with parsley.

Serves 4. About 323 kcal per serving

Green asparagus with lemon marinade

This light, easy-to-make dish is an ideal starter. While the asparagus is marinating, the rest of the meal can be prepared.

❶ Wash the asparagus. and remove the ends. Blanch the asparagus in boiling salted water with sugar and butter. Remove from the water, drain and arrange in a shallow dish.

❷ Wash the lemon in hot water, wipe dry and thinly grate the zest of half the lemon. Squeeze out the juice. Season the 3–4 tablespoons of lemon juice with salt and pepper and add the oil to make a marinade. Wash the chives, dry, chop finely and add to the marinade.

❸ Sprinkle the marinade and lemon zest over the asparagus and leave to stand for 2 hours. Garnish with lemon balm before serving.

Serves 4. About 171 kcal per serving

1 kg/2¼ lb green asparagus

salt

½ teaspoon sugar

1 teaspoon butter

juice and zest of 1 untreated lemon

freshly ground pepper

4 tablespoons sunflower oil

1 bunch chives

lemon balm as garnish

Asparagus pieces in chervil sauce

Use young, fresh sprigs of chervil. It can be found as early as May, just right for the asparagus season.

❶ Wash the potatoes, cook in their skins, peel and toss in 30 g/1 oz hot, melted butter just before serving.

❷ Peel the asparagus, remove the woody ends and cook in boiling salted water with 10 g/⅜ oz (2 teaspoons) butter until done.

❸ Fry the sunflower seeds in 10 g/⅜ oz (2 teaspoons) butter. Heat up the crème fraîche with 8 tablespoons asparagus cooking water and season with salt and pepper. Stir in half the sunflower seeds and chervil and heat up again.

❹ Remove the asparagus from the water, drain well and arrange on a serving dish. Pour the chervil sauce over the asparagus and sprinkle with the remaining sunflower seeds.

Serves 4. About 474 kcal per serving

1 kg/2¼ lb small potatoes

50 g/2 oz (4 tablespoons) butter

1 kg/2¼ lb white asparagus

salt

80 g/3 oz sunflower seeds

8 tablespoons crème fraîche

freshly ground white pepper

12 tablespoons chervil leaves

Flans and baked dishes

Here are yet more recipes which show the great versatility of asparagus and its ability to combine with other vegetables, with ham and cheese, and with pizza, puff and shortcrust pastry. The recipes include a number of international dishes such as Asparagus quiche (page 71) and Asparagus flan (page 58) and Asparagus soufflé (page 68), inspired by French cuisine, while Asparagus lasagne (see page 66), and Asparagus pizza with mascarpone (page 62) conjure up pictures of Italy. There are wonderful gratins prepared with potatoes (page 65), spinach (page 74) or broccoli (page 61). Asparagus in rolled oats (page 64) is a quite irresistible dish.

Asparagus gratin with bacon

This gratin is excellent with a sturdy white wine such as Gewürztraminer.

800 g/1¾ lb white asparagus

salt

sugar

1 teaspoon butter

450 g/1 lb puff pastry, frozen

150 g/5½ oz smoked bacon

130 g/1 oz mozzarella

3 eggs

125 ml/4 fl oz (½ cup) cream

300 ml/10 fl oz (1¼ cups) dry
    white wine

freshly ground pepper

1 teaspoon meat stock (broth)

curry powder to taste

1 tablespoon finely chopped
    chives

❶ Peel the asparagus, remove the woody ends and cut the asparagus stalks (stems) into pieces 2 cm/1¼ in long. Cook in boiling salted water with 1 pinch of sugar and butter for 15 minutes. Remove from the water and drain well.

❷ Put the defrosted puff pastry dough on a floured work-surface and roll out the same size as the spring-mould. Line the spring-mould with the rolled out dough, pressing the edge against the sides of the mould to a height of about 4 cm/1½ in. Arrange the asparagus in the pastry case.

❸ Cut the bacon into strips and fry lightly in the pan. Cut the mozzarella into thin slices. Put the bacon strips and mozzarella slices on the asparagus and bake in the oven pre-heated to 220°C (425°F), Gas mark 7 for about 10 minutes.

❹ Whisk the eggs into the cream then, add the white wine and meat stock (broth). Season with salt, pepper, a little sugar, and curry if desired. Pour the sauce over the gratin, sprinkle the chives on top and bake for a further 25 minutes.

Serves 4. About 1,013 kcal per serving

Asparagus in puff pastry

The puff pastry cases are decorated with a puff pastry heart-shape – a plesantly friendly detail for your guests.

❶ Peel the asparagus, remove the woody ends. Cook the asparagus on salted boiling water with a pinch of sugar and a little butter for about 10 minutes. Remove the asparagus from the water, drain well and divide into four portions. Wrap each portion in a slice of cheese and ham.

❷ Lightly roll out 4 defrosted layers separately on a floured work surface. Put an asparagus parcel on each piece of puff pastry. Brush white of egg on the edges of the pastry. Fold the pastry over the parcel, and press the edges together. Cut out four heart shapes from the remaining layer, brush one side with white of egg and press onto the puff pastry cases. Brush beaten egg yolk over all the puff pastry cases and bake in the oven pre-heated to 220°C (425°F), Gas mark 7 for 15 minutes.

❸ Mix the white wine and vinegar together and stir in the finely chopped onion, tarragon and basil, pepper. Boil for 5 minutes to reduce. Put the saucepan in a container of cold water, and beat the egg yolk into the mixture. Remove the saucepan from the cold water. Stir the melted but not hot butter into the sauce and season with salt, pepper and sugar.

Serves 4. About 682 kcal per serving

750 g/1½ lb white asparagus

salt

1 pinch sugar

butter

4 slices medium mature Gouda

4 slices cooked ham

5 slices puff pastry, frozen

1 egg white

yolk of 1 egg

For the sauce:

1 small onion

½ tablespoon tarragon leaves

½ tablespoon leaves of basil

freshly ground pepper

½ tablespoon white wine-vinegar

2 tablespoons dry, medium white wine

yolk of 1 egg

100 g/3½ oz (½ cup) butter

salt

pinch of sugar

Asparagus flan

Béchamel sauce is a component of many classic asparagus dishes because it enhances the delicate flavour of asparagus.

500 g/18 oz asparagus, mixed

salt

10 g/⅜ oz (2 teaspoons) butter

1 teaspoon sugar

500 ml/17 fl oz (2¼ cups) béchamel sauce (ready-made product)

100 g/3½ oz curd cheese

yolks of 2 eggs

100 g/3½ oz celeriac

2–3 teaspoons dill

freshly ground white pepper

300 g/11 oz puff pastry, frozen

flour for the work surface

❶ Peel the asparagus, remove the woody ends and cut the asparagus stalks (stems) into pieces 2 cm/¾ in long. Heat water in a large saucepan. As soon as the water boils, add the salt, butter and sugar. Add the asparagus and cook for about 10 minutes until done. Pour away the water and drain well.

❷ Mix the béchamel sauce, curd cheese and egg yolk in a bowl and stir until the mixture is creamy. Grate the cheese and add to the béchamel sauce together with the chopped dill. Stir well and season with white pepper.

❸ Rinse the flan tin in cold water and drain. Place the defrosted puff pastry on a floured work surface and roll out to the size of the flan tin. Line the flan tin with the dough and press the dough into along the edges. If necessary, cut off the excess dough with a flat knife. Pour the béchamel sauce into the flan tin and add the asparagus pieces, making sure that they are all covered by the sauce.

❹ Bake for about 20 minutes in the oven pre-heated to 200°C (400°F), Gas mark 6.

Serves 4. About 997 kcal per serving

Asparagus strudel

Although the word strudel immediately conjures up the image of the famous apple dessert, there is also a delicious savoury version.

800 g/1¾ lb green asparagus

400 g/14 oz white asparagus

salt

yolks of 4 egg

100 g/3½ oz quark

2 tablespoons flour

3 teaspoons cornflour (cornstarch)

freshly ground pepper

300 g/11 oz puff pastry, frozen

4 tablespoons breadcrumbs

30 g/1 oz (2 tablespoons) butter

250 ml/8 fl oz (1 cup) hollandaise sauce (made from packet mix, or following recipe page 122)

½ bunch parsley

❶ Wash the green asparagus, peel the white asparagus, remove the woody ends. Cut off and reserve the asparagus tips. Cook the rest in salted boiling water for 10 minutes. Remove from the water and drain well. Cut the asparagus stalks (stems) into small pieces and cook in salted water until very tender. Pour away the water and drain. Purée the asparagus very finely and leave to cool down in a bowl. Add the egg yolk, quark, flour and cornflour (cornstarch) and stir well. Season with salt and pepper and put in the refrigerator.

❷ Roll out the puff pastry very thin on a large tea towel and sprinkle with breadcrumbs. Spread the asparagus purée across two-thirds of the rolled out dough and put the asparagus tips on top. Brush the remaining third of the rolled out pastry with melted butter. Lifting the edge of the teatowel slightly, carefully roll up the dough.

❸ Place the strudel on the baking sheet, brush with melted butter and bake in the oven preheated to 180°C (350°F), Gas mark 4 for 50–60 minutes. Brush with more melted butter from time to time.

❹ Heat the hollandaise sauce following the instructions on the packet, or prepare according to the recipe and garnish with parsley. Serve with the strudel.

Serves 4. About 630 kcal per serving

Asparagus and broccoli gratin

This gratin also contains very tender veal escalopes making an attractive combined meat and vegetable dish.

800 g/1¾ lb white asparagus

salt

200 g/7 oz broccoli

4 veal escalopes (about 200 g/7 oz each)

freshly ground pepper

oil for cooking

225 ml/8 fl oz (1 cup) cream

50 g/2 oz (½ cup) flour

20 g/¾ oz (1½ tablespoons) butter

egg of 2 yolks

freshly grated nutmeg

100 g/3½ oz cooked ham

200 g/7 oz mozzarella

❶ Peel the asparagus and remove the woody ends. Cut the asparagus stalks (stems) into pieces 4 cm/1¼ in long. Add to boiling salted water and simmer for 17 minutes. Remove from the water and drain.

❷ Wash the broccoli and remove the stalks (stems). Cook the florets for 8 minutes in salted water over a low heat. Remove from the water and drain.

❸ Season the veal escalopes with salt and pepper and fry in the oil for 10 minutes.

❹ Heat the cream. Work the flour and butter into a dough. Stir the dough into the cream, little by little, and bring the mixture to the boil. Remove from the heat and stir in the egg yolk. Season the sauce with salt, pepper and nutmeg. Cut the ham into strips and add to the sauce together with asparagus and broccoli.

❺ Place the veal steaks in a gratin dish and cover with the vegetables. Slice the mozzarella and arrange on top of the vegetables. Brown lightly in the oven preheated to 200°–220°C (400°–425°F), Gas mark 6–7.

Serves 4. About 843 kcal per serving

Asparagus pizza with mascarpone

There is an endless variety of pizzas. Here is an asparagus one to try!

For the dough:

300 g/11 oz (3 cups) flour

20 g/¾ oz yeast

1 pinch sugar

½ teaspoon salt

3 tablespoons olive oil

For the topping:

500 g/18 oz green asparagus

salt

2 large onions

2 tablespoons olive oil

100 g/3½ oz smoked salmon, cut in thin slices

some flour

150 ml/5 fl oz (⅝ cup) sour cream

100 g/3½ oz mascarpone

2 tablespoons pine kernels

12 black olives

freshly ground pepper

❶ Put the flour in a bowl. Mix the yeast with 150 ml/5 fl oz (⅝ cup) warm water and sugar, stir until smooth and pour onto the flour. Add the salt, oil and about 50 ml/1½ fl oz (5 tablespoons) water and work into a smooth, homogenous dough. Sprinkle flour over the dough, cover and put in a warm place for 1 hour.

❷ Wash the asparagus and remove the woody ends. Blanch the asparagus in salted boiling water. Remove and drain. Peel the onions, cut into rings and fry briefly in olive oil. Cut the salmon slices into pieces.

❸ Put the dough on a floured work surface, knead again thoroughly and roll out thinly. Put on a well-oiled baking-sheet. Cover the dough with soured cream. Arrange the onions, asparagus, mascarpone, pine kernels and olives on the pizza. Season with salt and pepper and bake for 25 minutes in the oven pre-heated to 220°C (425°F), Gas mark 7. Finally, arrange the smoked salmon on the pizza once it is cooked.

Serves 4. About 765 kcal per serving

Asparagus in rolled oats

The crisp coating of rolled oats is an interesting variation on the traditional omelette adding an unusual dimension to the refined asparagus flavour.

For the batter:

2 eggs

80 g/3 oz (scant 1 cup) wheat flour

12 tablespoons porridge (rolled) oats

60 ml/2 fl oz (6 tablespoons) milk

60 ml/2 fl oz (6 tablespoons) mineral water

salt

butter

Further ingredients:

1 kg/2¼ lb white asparagus

salt

1 teaspoon sugar

250 g/9 oz mozzarella

2 tablespoons crème fraîche

½ bunch parsley

½ bunch chives

freshly ground pepper

1 tablespoon lemon juice

3 tablespoons sour cream

1 egg yolk

freshly grated nutmeg

3 tablespoons Parmesan cheese, freshly grated

❶ Mix the eggs, flour, 4 tablespoons porridge (rolled) oats, milk, mineral water and pinch of salt and work into a smooth batter. Allow to stand for ½ hour. Heat the butter in a pan, add 1 tablespoon rolled oats, then a little batter and make a total of 8 pancakes in this way.

❷ Peel the asparagus and remove the woody ends. Cook the asparagus in boiling salted water with a pinch of sugar for about 10 minutes. Cut the mozzarella into small cubes and stir into the crème fraîche together with the finely chopped parsley and chives. Season with salt, pepper, sugar and lemon juice.

❸ Stir the egg yolk into the sour cream, season with nutmeg, salt and pepper.

❹ Arrange the asparagus on the pancakes and top with a little cream and mozzarella. Roll up the pancakes and arrange in a greased gratin dish. Pour the sour cream mixture over the pancakes, sprinkle with Parmesan and brown for 12 minutes in the oven pre-heated to 200°C (400°F), Gas mark 6.

Serves 4. About 642 kcal per serving

Asparagus gratin with Parmesan

A gratin need not always mean potatoes! An asparagus gratin requires very few ingredients, takes very little time to prepare and is perfect as a starter or side dish.

❶ Wash the green asparagus, peel the white asparagus and remove the woody ends. Cook the asparagus in salted water with a pinch of sugar for about 10 minutes until done. Remove from the water and drain.

❷ Put the asparagus in a greased gratin dish, sprinkle with Parmesan and dot with flakes of herb butter. Brown under the preheated grill for 3 minutes.

Serves 4. About 392 kcal per serving

500 g/18 oz green asparagus

500 g/18 oz white asparagus

salt

1 pinch sugar

200 g/7 oz grated Parmesan

125 g/4½ oz (⅝ cup) herb butter

Potato and asparagus gratin

The addition of fresh asparagus adds a touch of luxury to the traditional potato gratin – perfect for an early summer dish.

❶ Wash the asparagus and remove the woody ends. Cook the asparagus in boiling salted water with sugar and 10 g/⅜ oz (2 teaspoons) butter for 10 minutes until done. Remove the asparagus from the water and drain.

❷ Peel the potatoes, cut into four and cook in salted water until done. Pour away the water. Let the potatoes to dry and mash with a potato masher. Add hot cream and stir into the potatoes. Season with salt, pepper and nutmeg. Leave to cool down a little and stir in the egg yolk.

❸ Put half the potato purée in well-greased gratin dish, followed by layers of half the ham, half the cheese, and all the asparagus, ending with a layer of the remaining ham. Put the remaining potato purée in a forcing bag with a star-shaped nozzle, and pipe across the ham in a lattice pattern. Dot with flakes of butter and sprinkle with the remaining cheese. Brown in the oven pre-heated to 220°C (425°F), Gas mark 7 for 15 minutes.

Serves 4. About 564 kcal per serving

500 g/18 oz green asparagus

salt

½ teaspoon sugar

50 g/2 oz (4 tablespoons) butter

800 g/1¾ lb cooked floury potatoes

125 ml/4 fl oz (½ cup) cream

freshly ground white pepper

freshly grated nutmeg

yolks of 2 eggs

fat for the mould

150 g/5½ oz cooked ham, diced

100 g/3½ oz (1 cup) grated Emmenthal

Asparagus lasagne

800 g/1¾ lb green asparagus

salt

1 pinch sugar

1 teaspoon butter

300 g/11 oz salmon

freshly ground pepper

10 sheets lasagne

150 g/5½ oz (1½ cups) grated Parmesan

1 tablespoon tarragon

For the béchamel sauce:

40 g/1½ oz (3 tablespoons) butter

3 tablespoons flour

300 ml/10 fl oz (1¼ cups) milk

50 ml/1½ fl oz (5 tablespoons) medium dry white wine

salt

freshly ground pepper

freshly grated nutmeg

1 tablespoon tarragon

Béchamel sauce is a classic component of asparagus dishes and lasagne, salmon and Parmesan perfectly complement their delicate flavour.

❶ Wash the asparagus thoroughly, remove the woody ends. Cook the asparagus in salted water with a pinch of sugar and 1 teaspoon butter for 3 minutes. Remove from the water and drain.

❷ Cut the salmon into cubes and season with salt and pepper.

❸ Cook the sheets of lasagne following the instructions on the packet. Remove the lasagne from the water, rinse under cold water and drain.

❹ To make the béchamel sauce: melt the butter and stir in the flour. Then little by little stir in the milk, wine and 400 ml/14 fl oz (1¾ cups) asparagus cooking water. Reduce the sauce while stirring constantly. Season with salt, pepper, nutmeg and tarragon.

❺ Now arrange alternate layers of béchamel sauce, lasagne, asparagus and salmon in a greased gratin dish, ending with a layer of lasagne sheets topped with the remaining béchamel sauce. Sprinkle with grated Parmesan and bake for 45 minutes in the oven pre-heated to 180°C (350°F), Gas mark 4. Remove from the oven and garnish with tarragon.

Serves 4. About 675 kcal per serving

Asparagus soufflé

A soufflé is much easier to make than many people believe. However, it is most important that all the ingredients should be prepared very quickly and that the soufflé should be served as soon as it is ready. It is vital that the oven door should not be opened during the first half hour; if it is, the soufflé will collapse.

❶ Wash the asparagus, remove the woody ends and put 4 asparagus stalks (stems) to one side. Cut the rest of the asparagus into pieces 1 cm/⅜ in long. Simmer the asparagus pieces gently in salted water with sugar for 10 minutes until done. Remove from the water, drain and separate the tips from the rest of the asparagus pieces.

❷ Melt the butter, stir in the flour and brown lightly. Add the milk, stirring constantly and allow to thicken. Stir in the vegetable stock (broth). Season with salt, nutmeg and pepper. Allow the sauce to cool down a little.

❸ Separate the eggs. Stir in the finely chopped parsley, grated cheese and egg yolk. Slice the raw asparagus very finely and stir into the sauce. Add a pinch of salt to the egg whites, beat vigorously to form stiff peaks. Fold gently into the sauce.

❹ Put the asparagus pieces in a well-greased gratin dish. Pour in the soufflé mixture and bake on the middle shelf for 25–30 minutes in the oven pre-heated to 220°C (425°F), Gas mark 7.

❺ Remove the soufflé from the oven. Garnish with the asparagus tips.

Serves 4. About 325 kcal per serving

500 g/18 oz green asparagus

salt

1 pinch sugar

45 g/1½ oz (3 tablespoons) butter

45 g/1½ oz (½ cup) flour

250 ml/8 fl oz (1 cup) milk

1 teaspoon vegetable stock (broth)

freshly grated nutmeg

freshly ground pepper

3 eggs

6 tablespoons parsley

100 g/3½ oz (1 cup) grated Emmenthal

fat for the mould

Asparagus crêpe gratin

Serve this asparagus crepe gratin with crusty French bread or buttered toast.

❶ Peel the asparagus, remove the woody ends and cook the asparagus in boiling salted water with a pinch of sugar for 10 minutes until done. Remove from the water and drain.

❷ To make the batter: add some water to the flour and stir ro make a smooth mixture. Add the eggs and whisk. Season with salt and pepper. Fry four crepes in the hot clarified butter.

❸ Roll up the asparagus in the crepes. Place in a greased gratin dish and sprinkle with cheese. Beat the cream and egg yolk together and pour over the crepes. Brown for 20 minutes in the oven pre-heated to 220°C (425°F), Gas mark 7. Remove from the oven and garnish with parsley.

Serves 4. About 441 kcal per serving

1 kg/2¼ lb white asparagus

salt

1 pinch sugar

1 teaspoon butter

fat for the mould

4 tablespoons grated Parmesan

125 ml/4 fl oz (½ cup) cream

yolk of 1 egg

1 tablespoon chopped parsley

For the batter:

1 tablespoon flour

6 eggs

salt

freshly ground pepper

clarified butter for frying

Asparagus gratin

The Gorgonzola adds a subtle touch to this dish. The Gorgonzola can be replaced with other blue cheeses, such as Roquefort which is milder but saltier than Gorgonzola.

❶ Peel the asparagus, remove the woody ends. Cook the asparagus in salted water with a pinch of sugar and a little butter for 10 minutes until done. Remove the asparagus from the water, drain and put in a well buttered gratin dish.

❷ Blanch the tomatoes, skin and chop up. Peel the onion, chop finely and braise lightly in the hot butter together with the chopped tomatoes. Add the basil, season with salt and pepper and pour the sauce over the asparagus.

❸ Cut the cheese into small cubes, stir into the crème fraîche and pour over the tomatoes and asparagus. Brown under the pre-heated oven grill for about 5 minutes.

Serves 4. About 302 kcal per serving

2 kg/4½ lb white asparagus

salt

1 pinch sugar

butter

3 tomatoes

2 onion

2–3 tablespoons finely chopped basil

freshly ground pepper

150 g/5½ oz Gorgonzola

3 tablespoons crème fraîche

Asparagus quiche

Originally a characteristic, nourishing speciality from the Lorraine region of France, the quiche has become a light, delicate dish made with a wide variety of ingredients.

❶ Mix the flour, egg yolk, clarified butter and 4 tablespoons water and work into a smooth dough and leave to rest in the refrigerator for 30 minutes.

❷ Wash the green asparagus, peel the white asparagus and remove the woody ends. Cut the asparagus stalks (stems) into pieces 5 cm/2 in long and simmer gently in the vegetable stock (broth) for 5 minutes. Remove from the stock (broth) and drain well.

❸ Cut the boiled ham into strips. Mix together the sour cream, eggs, finely chopped chervil, cheese, salt, pepper and nutmeg and stir well. Wash the cherry tomatoes and cut them in half.

❹ Roll out the dough thinly on a floured work surface, line a flan tin with it and bake for 10 minutes in the oven pre-heated to 190°C (375°F), Gas mark 5. Remove from the oven and arrange the asparagus, tomatoes and ham in the pastry case. Pour the sour cream mixture on top and bake for another 25–30 minutes.

Serves 4. About 924 kcal per serving

For the pastry:

200 g/7 oz (2 cups) flour

½ teaspoon salt

yolks of 2 eggs

125 g/4½ oz (⅝ cup) clarified butter

For the topping:

250 g/9 oz green asparagus

500 g/18 oz white asparagus

200 ml/7 fl oz (⅞ cup) vegetable stock (broth)

150 g/5½ oz cooked ham

150 ml/5 fl oz (⅝ cup) sour cream

4 eggs

1 bunch chervil

100 g/3½ oz (1 cup) grated Emmenthal

salt

pepper

freshly grated nutmeg

125 g/4½ oz cherry tomatoes

Asparagus flan

1.5 kg/3 lb white asparagus

salt

4 onions

750 g/1½ lb potatoes

500 g/18 oz cooked ham

6 tomatoes

tarragon

freshly ground pepper

225 ml/8 fl oz (2 cups) cream

6 eggs

300 g/11 oz grated Gouda

butter

It is important to use green asparagus for this nourishing asparagus and potato flan.

❶ Peel the asparagus, remove the woody ends and cook the asparagus in salted water for 10 minutes. Remove from the water and drain thoroughly.

❷ Peel the onions and potatoes. Dice the ham and onions. Slice the potatoes and tomatoes.

❸ Take half the potatoes, asparagus, ham, tomatoes and onions and arrange in layers in the gratin dish, then repeat the layers in the same order with the remaining ingredients. Sprinkle each layer with tarragon, salt and pepper.

❹ Beat the eggs into the cream and pour over the layered vegetables, sprinkle with Gouda and dot with flakes of butter. Cook in the oven at 180°C (350°F), Gas mark 4 for 1½ hours.

Serves 4. About 1.260 kcal per serving

Asparagus and crab parcels

200 g/7 oz white asparagus

salt

400 g/14 oz crab meat

100 g/3½ oz (1 cup) chopped almonds

300 ml/10 fl oz (1¼ cups) double cream cheese with herbs

2 tablespoons breadcrumbs

2 tablespoons dill, coarsely chopped

freshly ground pepper

600 g/1¼ lb puff pastry, frozen

flour for the work surface

yolks of 2 eggs

Asparagus need not always be the main ingredient in a dish; in this recipe, the main ingredient is crab, but it does not diminish the delicate flavour of the asparagus in any way.

❶ Peel the asparagus and remove the woody ends. Cut the asparagus into pieces 2 cm/1¼ in long. Cook in salted water for 10 minutes until done. Remove from the water and drain.

❷ Mix together the asparagus, crab, almonds, cheese flavoured with herbs, breadcrumbs and dill. Season with salt and pepper.

❸ Separate the puff pastry into single layers and roll out square on a floured work surface. Put some of the crab-asparagus mixture on each square layer. Wet the edges of the squares with water and fold it to make triangles. Brush egg yolk on the pastry cases and bake for 20 minutes in the oven pre-heated to 200°C (400°F), Gas mark 6.

Serves 4. About 1,185 kcal per serving

Asparagus and ham gratin

The classic combination of asparagus and ham is complemented in this gratin by a delicious cream cheese sauce.

1 kg/2¼ lb white asparagus

salt

1 pinch sugar

100 g/3½ oz (½ cup) butter

8 thick slices cooked ham

1 tablespoon flour

1 egg yolks

freshly ground pepper

freshly grated nutmeg

50 g/2 oz (1/3 cup) grated Parmesan

2 tablespoons chopped parsley

❶ Peel the asparagus, remove the woody ends and cook in boiling salted water with sugar and 10 g/⅜ oz (2 teaspoons) butter for 10 minutes until done. Remove from the water, drain and roll up in ham in individual portions.

❷ Heat 40 g/1½ oz (3 tablespoons) butter in a saucepan, stir in flour and add 250 ml/8 fl oz (1 cup) asparagus stock (broth), stirring constantly. Cook for 5 minutes and remove from the heat. Thicken the sauce with the egg yolk. Season with salt, pepper and nutmeg.

❸ Place the ham and asparagus rolls in a greased gratin dish and pour the sauce on top. Sprinkle with Parmesan and dot a few flakes of butter on top. Bake for 20 minutes in the oven pre-heated to 220°C (425°F), Gas mark 7. Remove from the oven and garnish with parsley.

Serves 4. About 392 kcal per serving

Asparagus gratin on a bed of spinach

The white asparagus and green spinach, topped with Gruyère, is both a delightful visual combination and a tasty, nourishing dish.

2 kg/4½ lb white asparagus

salt

1 pinch sugar

90 g/3 oz (6 tablespoons) butter

800 g/1¾ lb leaf spinach

450 g/1 lb Gruyère, sliced

❶ Peel the asparagus, remove the woody ends and cook the asparagus in boiling salted water with a pinch of sugar and 10 g/⅜ oz (2 teaspoons) butter for 10 minutes until done.

❷ Wash the spinach, blanch in boiling salted water, remove, drain and press a little to squeeze out any remaining water. Butter an ovenproof dish, put half the spinach on top and cover with the asparagus.

❸ Cut the remaining spinach into strips and put on top of the asparagus, dot some flakes of butter on top and cover with the slices of Gruyère. Bake on the lowest shelf of the oven pre-heated to 220°C/425°F (gas 7). After about 15 minutes, put under the grill for a further 3 minutes until golden brown.

Serves 4. About 670 kcal per serving

Fish and seafood dishes

Almost all the culinary delights offered by rivers and the sea combines very successfully with asparagus, be it salmon or crabs from the North Sea, shrimps or sole from more southerly regions, or trout and zander from lakes and rivers. Some of these dishes are quick and easy to prepare, such as the Green asparagus with rolled sole (page 78), Smoked trout fillets with asparagus (page 91) or Salmon with green asparagus sauce (page 82). Slightly more time consuming are Asparagus ragout with shrimps (page 84), Cod with asparagus (page 86) and Baked catfish with asparagus (page 85). A very special combination which is remarkably easy to make is Asparagus with salmon steak and shrimps (page 92).

Green asparagus with salmon trout

This recipe uses every part of the orange, the juice, zest and thin slices of orange. It also includes orange-coloured pepper, giving the dish a very exotic appearance.

1 kg/2¼ lb green asparagus

salt

1 pinch sugar

2 salmon trout (about 400 g/14 oz each)

4 tablespoons lemon juice

2 untreated oranges

30 g/1 oz hollandaise sauce mix

125 g/4½ oz (⅝ cups) butter

ground orange pepper

1 bunch dill

dill umbels for garnish

❶ Wash the asparagus and remove the woody ends. Cook the asparagus in gently simmering salted water with sugar for 12 minutes until done.

❷ Wash the sea trout, wipe dry and cook in gently simmering salted water with lemon juice for about 10 minutes until done. Divide into portions and put aside in a warm place.

❸ Grate the zest of an orange and squeeze to obtain the juice. Bring the orange juice to the boil with 125 ml/4 fl oz (1 cup) water, stir in the hollandaise sauce mix and bring to the boil again. Stir flakes of butter, little by little, into the sauce. Add the orange zest and season with the salt and orange pepper.

❹ Remove the asparagus from the water and drain. Arrange on four plates with the fish and pour the hollandaise on top. Garnish with slices of orange, dill and dill flowers.

Serves 4. About 534 kcal per serving

Green asparagus with rolled sole

This light asparagus dish is delicious served with potatoes, or as a change with cooked rice

1.5 kg/3 lb green asparagus

salt

8 slices smoked cured loin of pork

8 fillets of sole (about 100 g/3½ oz each)

juice of 1 lemon

250 ml/8 fl oz (1 cup) hollandaise sauce (packet mix or recipe page 122)

❶ Wash the asparagus, remove the woody ends and cook in gently simmering salted water for 8–10 minutes until done.

❷ Place the slices of pork loin on the smooth side of the sole fillets, roll up and secure. Bring the salted water and lemon juice to the boil, add the rolled sole and pork and simmer for 12 minutes.

❸ Heat up the hollandaise sauce. Remove the asparagus and rolled sole and pork from the water and drain. Arrange on plates and pour the hollandaise sauce on top.

Serves 4. About 456 kcal per serving

Asparagus and salmon fillet gratin

White and green asparagus are used in this recipe, giving a particular flavour as well as a pleasing colour contrast.

600 g/1¼ lb small potatoes

500 g/18 oz green asparagus

500 g/18 oz white asparagus

salt

15 g/½ oz (1 tablespoon) butter

1 tablespoon flour

125 ml/4 fl oz (½ cup) cream

freshly ground pepper

½ bunch parsley

600 g/1¼ lb salmon fillets

freshly ground pepper

4 slices medium mature Gouda

1 untreated lemon

½ bunch dill

❶ Wash the potatoes, peel and boil. Wash the green asparagus, peel the white asparagus and remove the woody ends. Boil the woody ends and peelings for 15 minutes in 1 litre/1¾ pints (4½ cups) salted water. Strain the asparagus stock (broth) through a sieve into a second saucepan and bring to the boil again. Cook the white asparagus for 15 minutes and the green asparagus for 5 minutes in this stock (broth) until done.

❷ Heat the butter, stir in the flour and add 125 ml/4 fl oz (1 cup) asparagus stock (broth). Add the cream. Season with salt and pepper and bring back to the boil.

❸ Drain the potatoes, let them dry and add to the sauce. Sprinkle with finely chopped parsley.

❹ Wash the salmon fillets. Season with salt and pepper.

❺ Remove the asparagus from the water, drain and arrange on the plates with salmon. Put a slice of Gouda on each salmon fillet and brown briefly under the grill. Garnish with pieces of lemon and dill.

Serves 4. About 684 kcal per serving

Asparagus omelette with smoked salmon

1 kg/2¼ lb white asparagus

salt

1 pinch sugar

1 teaspoon butter

For the hollandaise sauce with herbs:

1 shallot

5 white peppercorns

1 tablespoon white wine-vinegar

yolks of 3 eggs

250 g/9 oz (1¼ cups) butter

salt

freshly ground pepper

1 tablespoon lemon juice

2 tablespoons finely chopped
   parsley

2 tablespoons finely chopped dill

For the omelettes:

8 eggs

4 tablespoons cream

salt

freshly ground pepper

freshly grated nutmeg

40 g/1½ oz (3 tablespoons) butter

300 g/11 oz smoked salmon in
   thin slices

The home-made hollandaise sauce with herbs gives the dish a delicious special touch.

❶ Peel the asparagus, remove the woody ends and boil in salted water with a pinch of sugar and a teaspoon of butter for 20 minutes until done.

❷ To make the herb hollandaise sauce: peel the shallots and chop finely. Add to the crushed peppercorns, vinegar and 5 tablespoons of water and boil to reduce it slightly. Rub through a fine sieve into a bowl, then beat in the egg yolk. Put the bowl in a container of hot water. Whisk the shallot and egg mixture continuously until it is creamy and thick. Remove the bowl from the hot water container and add melted butter – not too hot – while stirring constantly. Season with salt, pepper and lemon juice and stir in the chopped herbs.

❸ For the omelette, beat the eggs and cream together. Season with salt, pepper and nutmeg and make four omelettes in butter.

❹ Remove the asparagus from the water and drain. Stuff the omelette with asparagus, salmon and hollandaise sauce with herbs.

Serves 4. About 952 kcal per serving

Salmon with green asparagus sauce

This mouth-watering salmon and asparagus dish is delicious served with new potatoes or wild rice.

500 g/18 oz green asparagus

salt

225 ml/8 fl oz (1 cup) cream

2 tablespoons crème fraîche

100 ml/3½ oz (scant ½ cup) dry white wine

freshly ground white pepper

4 salmon slices (about 200 g/7 oz each)

juice of ½ lemon

200 ml/7 fl oz (⅞ cup) vegetable stock (broth)

❶ Wash the asparagus and remove the woody ends. Cook the asparagus in salted water for 15–20 minutes until done. Remove from the water and drain.

❷ Heat the cream, add the crème fraîche and wine and stir until the mixture is creamy. Season with salt and pepper, add the asparagus.

❸ Sprinkle lemon juice on the salmon slices and cook in the hot vegetable stock (broth) for 6–8 minutes.

❹ Remove from the vegetable stock (broth) and garnish with asparagus sauce.

Serves 4. About 622 kcal per serving

Zander fillet with asparagus

The zander fillet and asparagus are delicious served with little new potatoes, peeled and fried lightly in a little melted butter.

1 kg/2¼ lb green asparagus

salt

2 lemon slices

15 g/½ oz (1 tablespoon) butter

1 teaspoon sugar

6 large tomatoes

4 tablespoons basil

2 tablespoons balsamic vinegar

8 tablespoons olive oil

freshly ground pepper

600 g/1¼ lb zander fillet

8 tablespoons lemon juice

4 tablespoons flour

❶ Wash the asparagus and remove the woody ends. Cook the asparagus in gently simmering salted water with 2 slices of lemon, butter and sugar for 10 minutes until done.

❷ Blanch the tomatoes in boiling water, peel, cut in half and remove the seeds. Cut into small cubes. Mix together the basil, vinegar, 6 tablespoons olive oil, salt and pepper and stir until smooth. Add the diced tomatoes.

❸ Sprinkle lemon juice on the zander fillets and season with salt, pepper. Coat in flour and fry in very hot olive oil on both sides for 2 minutes until golden brown.

❹ Remove the asparagus from the water, drain and arrange on plates with the zander fillets. Pour a little tomato vinaigrette over and serve the rest separately.

Serves 4. About 453 kcal per serving

Asparagus prawn (shrimp) ragout

750 g/1½ lb white asparagus

750 g/1½ lb green asparagus

salt

12 prawns (shrimps), peeled

2 tablespoons lemon juice

freshly ground white pepper

2 onions

70 g/3 oz (6 tablespoons) ice-cold butter

80 g/3 oz mushroom

4 sprigs tarragon

1 bunch dill

400 ml/14 fl oz (1¾ cups) fish stock (broth)

75 ml/2½ fl oz (8 tablespoons) dry white wine

600 ml/1 pint (2½ cups) cream

2 teaspoons sugar

1 tablespoon flour

This shellfish dish has a particularly delicate taste.

❶ Peel the white asparagus, wash the green asparagus and remove the woody ends. Cook the woody ends and peelings in 2 litres/3½ pints (9 cups) salted water for about 30 minutes until the liquid has been reduced by almost one-third. Wash the prawns (shrimps) and sprinkle with lemon juice, season with salt and pepper and leave to stand for a while.

❷ Peel the onions and cut each into eight. Melt 1 tablespoon butter in a pan and sweat the onions until transparent. Clean and wash the mushrooms, cut in half, add to the onions together with the tarragon leaves and 1 tablespoon finely chopped dill and simmer for 3–5 minutes.

❸ Strain the asparagus stock (broth) through a sieve into another saucepan. Pour 1 litre/1¾ pints (4½ cups) asparagus stock (broth), fish stock (broth) and white wine onto the mushrooms. Stir in the cream and reduce the mixture to 500 ml/17 fl oz (2¼ cups) in all.

❹ Cut the asparagus into pieces 5 cm/2 in long. Bring the remaining asparagus stock (broth) to the boil and cook the white asparagus in it together with 1 tablespoon butter, sugar and salt for about 10 minutes, the green asparagus for about 5 minutes until done.

❺ Strain the reduced asparagus-mushroom mixture through a sieve into a large saucepan. Stir a little water into the flour and stir it into this mixture, using a whisk, and bring to the boil. Add ice-cold flakes of butter and whisk until foamy.

❻ Add the prawns (shrimps) and asparagus to this mixture and heat again, but do not bring to the boil. Season with salt and butter and garnish with the rest of the dill.

Serves 4. About 765 kcal per serving

Baked catfish
with asparagus

If you do not have much time to cook, you can also make this dish with tinned asparagus and instant mashed potato.

1 Wash and boil the potatoes. Peel the asparagus, remove the woody ends and cook in boiling salted water with a pinch of sugar and 10 g/⅜ oz (2 teaspoons) butter for 10 minutes until done.

2 Season the fish with salt and simmer gently in the fish stock (broth) and wine for 10 minutes.

3 When the potatoes are cooked, pour away the water, peel and mash or rub through a food mill. Add milk and 20 g/¾ oz (1½ tablespoons) butter and whisk, beat or mash to obtain a creamy mixture. Season with salt.

4 Add a little fish stock (broth) to the white fish sauce. Remove the asparagus from the water, drain and arrange in a well greased gratin dish. Put the fish and crab meat on top and pour the fish sauce over. Sprinkle with Parmesan and dot a few butter flakes on top. Arrange the potato purée around the fish and asparagus; brush with egg yolk. Brown under medium heat for 15 minutes.

Serves 4. About 763 kcal per serving

750 g/1½ lb floury potatoes

350 g/12 oz white asparagus

salt

1 pinch sugar

80 g/3 oz (6 tablespoons) butter

4 slices catfish
  (about 150 g/5½ oz each)

250 ml/8 fl oz (1 cup) fish stock
  (broth)

250 ml/8 fl oz (1 cup) dry white
  wine

250 ml/8 fl oz (1 cup) milk

100 ml/3½ fl oz (scant ½ cup)
  white fish sauce

50 g/2 oz crab meat

60 g/2 oz (⅓ cup) grated
  Parmesan

yolks of 2 eggs

Cod with asparagus

Instead of cod, other sea or freshwater fish can be used, such as rose fish, white halibut, turbot or salmon trout.

1 kg/2¼ lb green asparagus

salt

1 untreated lemon

15 g/½ oz (1 tablespoon) butter

½ teaspoon sugar

4 cod fillets
   (about 200 g/7 oz each)

freshly ground white pepper

2 tablespoons flour

2 tablespoons oil

½ bunch dill

For the wine and cream sauce:

4 medium shallots

80 g/3 oz (6 tablespoons) butter

200 ml/7 fl oz (⅞ cup) medium
   dry Riesling

300 ml/10 fl oz (1¼ cups) cream

salt

freshly ground pepper

1 pinch sugar

❶ Wash the asparagus and remove the woody ends. Cook the asparagus in gently simmering salted water with a sliced lemon, butter, salt and sugar for 10–15 minutes until done. Remove from the water, drain and keep in a warm place.

❷ Wash the cod fillets, wipe dry, season with salt and pepper, coat in flour and fry in oil for 15 minutes until golden brown.

❸ For the cream and wine sauce: peel the shallots, chop finely and sweat in 40 g/1½ oz (3 tablespoons) melted butter until transparent. Add the Riesling and reduce the liquid to about one-third. Add the cream and reduce the sauce again to half. Add 100 ml/3½ fl oz (scant ½ cup) asparagus stock (broth), cook for 2–3 minutes, stir to obtain a smooth texture and beat 40 g/1½ oz (3 tablespoons) butter into the sauce, using a whisk. Season with salt, pepper and sugar.

❹ Arrange the asparagus on plates and pour the wine and cream sauce over them, put the cod fillet on top and garnish with dill.

Serves 4. About 711 kcal per serving

Green asparagus with crab

Chilli is terribly hot! It is therefore advisable to prepare them under cold running water or to wear kitchen gloves.

❶ Wash the asparagus and remove the woody ends. Cook the asparagus in gently simmering salted water for 5 minutes until done. Remove from the water, run under cold water, drain and cut into pieces.

❷ Wash the mangetouts (snow peas), peel and slice the carrots and blanch both in boiling salted water for 2 minutes. Remove from the water, run under cold water and drain.

❸ Wash the courgettes (zucchini), cut off the stalks (stems), cut in half lengthways and slice thinly and sprinkle a little salt on top. Wash the chilli pepper, cut open lengthways and remove the stalk and white membrane from the inside. Cut into thin rings.

❹ Fry the carrots and asparagus in 2 tablespoons soya oil for 2–3 minutes, then add the crushed garlic, chilli, courgettes (zucchini), mangetouts (snow peas) and crab. Season with soya sauce and pepper and garnish with finely chopped chervil.

Serves 4. About 224 kcal per serving

750 g/1½ lb asparagus

salt

150 g/5½ oz mangetouts (snow peas)

175 g/6 oz carrots

3 small courgettes (zucchini)

1 chilli pod

2 tablespoons soya oil

2 clove garlic

300 g/11 oz crab meat

3 tablespoons soya sauce

freshly ground pepper

1 bunch chervil

Angler fish and asparagus in saffron sauce

Angler is quite a rare fish which often has to be ordered from the fishmonger. Cod or salmon trout may be used as an alternative.

❶ Peel the white asparagus, wash the green asparagus and remove the woody ends. Cook the white asparagus for 20 minutes and the green asparagus for 10 minutes in simmering salted water with sugar until done. Remove from the water, drain and keep warm in the oven at the lowest possible setting.

❷ Rinse the fish fillet, wipe dry and cut into slices 2 cm/¾ in thick. Sprinkle with lemon juice and a little salt. Coat in flour. Fry in butter for 2–3 minutes on each side, remove from the pan and keep warm in the oven.

❸ Add the cream to the pan and stir into the cooking fat. Add 1 cup of asparagus stock (broth), saffron and peas. Reduce the liquid a little. Pour in the vegetable stock (broth), season with salt and stir the finely chopped parsley into the sauce.

❹ Arrange the asparagus on plates, pour the sauce over and put the fish next to it.

Serves 4. About 406 kcal per serving

300 g/11 oz white asparagus

300 g/11 oz green asparagus

salt

½ teaspoon sugar

600 g/1¼ lb angler fish fillets

5 teaspoons lemon juice

2 tablespoons flour

45 g/1½ oz (3 tablespoons) butter

225 ml/8 fl oz (1 cup) cream

a few threads of saffron

125 g/4½ oz peas

1 teaspoon vegetable stock (broth)

1 bunch parsley

Plaice fillets with asparagus on a bed of watercress

Plaice is particularly good during the asparagus season.

❶ Grate the zest of 2 lemons and put to one side. Rinse the plaice fillets under cold water, wipe dry and sprinkle with the juice of 2 lemons. Leave to stand for a while.

❷ Peel the asparagus and remove the woody ends. Cook the asparagus in boiling salted water with sugar and 25 g/1 oz (2 tablespoons) butter for 15 minutes until done.

❸ Season the plaice fillets with salt and pepper and fry in 50 g/2 oz (4 tablespoons) butter over medium heat for 2 minutes on each side. Remove from the pan and keep in a warm place.

❹ Deglaze the cooking juices with wine and 8 tablespoons asparagus and cook to reduce. Stir in the double cream and lemon zest. Season with salt and pepper and stir in the watercress leaves.

❺ Remove the asparagus from the water, drain and arrange on the plates with the plaice fillets. Pour the cress sauce on top and garnish with lemon quarters.

Serves 4. About 810 kcal per serving

4 untreated lemons
1 kg/2¼ lb fillets of plaice
2 kg/4½ lb white asparagus
salt
1 teaspoon sugar
80 g/3 oz (6 tablespoons) butter
freshly ground pepper
250 ml/8 fl oz (1 cup) white wine
300 g/11 oz (1¼ cups) double cream
2 bunches watercress

Asparagus with prawn (shrimp) and orange sauce

This delicious casserole of asparagus and prawns (shrimps) with delicate hints of orange is delicious served with white tagliatelle.

❶ Peel the asparagus and remove the woody ends. Wash the mangetouts (snow peas), trim as needed and cut into pieces. Wash the prawns (shrimps) and wipe them dry.

❷ Cook the asparagus in boiling salted water with sugar and butter for 10 minutes until done. Add the mangetouts (snow peas) and cook for another 10 minutes.

❸ Peel the onion, chop finely and fry in 20 g/¾ oz (1½ tablespoons) crab butter. Pour in the lobster stock (broth), simmer for 10 minutes. Add the cream, vermouth, orange juice and orange zest. Bring to the boil, stir in the thickening and season with salt and pepper.

❹ Fry the prawns (shrimps) in the remaining fat for about 3 minutes and add to the sauce. Remove the asparagus and mangetouts (snow peas) from the water and drain. Put in a bowl and pour the ragout on top.

Serves 4. About 421 kcal per serving

1.5 kg/3 lb white asparagus

200 g/7 oz mangetouts (snow peas)

16 large prawns (shrimps), raw, without head and peeled

salt

sugar

10 g/⅜ oz (2 teaspoons) butter

1 onion

50 g/2 oz (4 tablespoons) crab butter

400 ml/14 fl oz (1¾ cups) lobster stock (broth)

100 ml/3½ oz (scant ½ cup) cream

50 ml/1½ fl oz (6 tablespoons) vermouth

3 tablespoons orange juice

zest of 1 untreated orange

3 tablespoons sauce thickening

freshly ground pepper

Smoked trout fillets with asparagus

This dish of smoked fillets of trout is prepared in no time at all.

❶ Peel the asparagus and remove the woody ends. Cook in boiling salted water with butter and sugar for about 20 minutes until done.

❷ Mix the quark, crème fraîche, oil and two-thirds of the cress leaves and liquidize in a blender until the mixture acquires a creamy texture. Add the remaining cress leaves to this sauce and season with salt, pepper and lemon juice.

❸ Remove the asparagus from the water, drain and arrange on the plates with the trout fillets. Pour the cress sauce on top or serve separately.

Serves 4. About 367 kcal per serving

1.5 kg/3 lb white asparagus

salt

1 teaspoon butter

1 pinch sugar

125 g/4½ oz quark

3 tablespoons crème fraîche

1 teaspoon oil

1 small box cress

freshly ground white pepper

2 tablespoons lemon juice

4 smoked trout fillets (about 150 g/5½ oz each)

Asparagus with salmon steak and prawns (shrimp)

This dish of asparagus, salmon and shrimps is an exquisite combination of delicate ingredients. It is delicious served with white bread or small new potatoes.

1.5 kg/3 lb white asparagus

salt

4 salmon steaks
(about 150 g/5½ oz each)

freshly ground pepper

2 tablespoons flour

40 g/1½ oz (3 tablespoons) butter

200 g/7 oz prawns (shrimps)

250 ml/8 fl oz (1 cup) hollandaise
sauce (packet mix, or recipe
page 122)

❶ Peel the asparagus and remove the woody ends. Cook the asparagus in boiling salted water for 20-30 minutes until done.

❷ Season the salmon with salt and pepper, coat in flour and fry on each side for 3–4 minutes in butter. Add the prawns (shrimps) and heat again.

❸ Heat the hollandaise sauce.

❹ Remove the asparagus from the water, drain and arrange on the plates with the salmon and prawns (shrimps). Pour the sauce on top.

Serves 4. About 657 kcal per serving

River trout with asparagus cream sauce

River trout is a fresh water fish that prefers cold waters and is therefore found mainly in the regions of Northern Europe and the Alps.

1 kg/2¼ lb white asparagus

salt

1 pinch sugar

85 g/3 oz (6 tablespoons) butter

85 g/3 oz (scant 1 cup) flour

225 ml/8 fl oz (1 cup) cream

freshly ground pepper

4 river trout fillets
(about 200 g/7 oz each)

❶ Peel the asparagus and remove the woody ends. Cut the asparagus stalks (stems) into pieces 2 cm/1¼ in long. Cook briefly in salted water with sugar. Remove the saucepan from the flame and leave the asparagus standing in the stock (broth) for about 15 minutes.

❷ Melt 35 g/1¼ oz (2½ tablespoons) butter. Stir in 35 g/1¼ oz (5 tablespoons) flour, pour in 250 ml/8 fl oz (1 cup) asparagus stock (broth), add the cream and stir. Reduce to obtain a thick consistency. Season with salt and pepper.

❸ Coat the river trout fillets in the remaining flour and fry in the hot, foaming butter for 5 minutes on each side.

❹ Remove the asparagus from the water and drain. Arrange on the plates together with the river trout. Pour the sauce on top.

Serves 4. About 770 kcal per serving

Poultry and meat dishes

It does not matter what kind of meat you prefer, or whether meat or asparagus is the main ingredient; the range of dishes combining meat and asparagus is endless. Excellent for lighter meals are Asparagus and chicken breast vol-au-vents (page 110) or the recipe for Veal medallions with asparagus (page 101). The Gratin of asparagus with smoked loin of pork (page 100) is more substantial, while the Asparagus, bean and meat gratin, enriched with bacon (page 98) will satisfy the heartiest appetite. The Rabbit fillet with green asparagus (page 97) will appeal to those who like spicy Oriental cuisine.

Asparagus with chicken breasts and creamed chervil

Although it takes some time, this delicious dish is quite easy to make.

1 kg/2¼ lb green asparagus

1 kg/2¼ lb white asparagus

salt

sugar

20 g/¾ oz (1½ tablespoons) butter

3 chicken breasts with skin and bone (about 500 g/18 oz each)

zest of 1 untreated lemon

freshly ground pepper

juice of 1½ lemons

2 tablespoons oil

2 shallots

225 ml/8 fl oz (1 cup) cream

10 g/⅜ oz (1½ tablespoons) flour

1 bunch chervil

❶ Wash the green asparagus, peel the white asparagus and remove the woody ends. Cook the woody ends and peelings for 15 minutes in salted water with sugar and 10 g/⅜ oz (2 teaspoons) butter. Strain the asparagus stock (broth) into another saucepan, putting aside 400 ml/14 fl oz (1¾ cups).

❷ Wash the chicken breasts, wipe dry, loosen the skin a little and rub some lemon zest onto the meat under the skin. Season the chicken breasts with salt and pepper, sprinkle with lemon juice and cook for about 40 minutes in oil. Remove the bones before serving.

❸ Bring the rest of the asparagus stock (broth) to the boil, add more water if necessary and cook the white asparagus in it for 20 minutes, and the green asparagus for 8 minutes until tender.

❹ Peel and chop the shallots. Cook for 10 minutes in the reserved 400 ml/14 fl oz (1¾ cups) asparagus stock (broth) together with the cream and remaining lemon juice in an uncovered saucepan. Strain through a sieve into another saucepan.

❺ Work the flour and remaining butter into a small ball of dough. Crumble bit by bit into the sauce and simmer for 3 minutes. Stir in the finely chopped chervil. Season with salt and pepper and whisk until foamy.

Serves 4. About 650 kcal per serving

Rabbit fillet with green asparagus

A recipe which is very much inspired by Oriental cuisine, so some of the ingredients may only be found in Oriental food shops.

1 kg/2¼ lb green asparagus

5 tablespoons groundnut oil

salt

freshly ground pepper

1 tablespoon Oriental mixed herbs

2 tablespoons sesame oil

4 rabbit fillets (about 100 g/3½ oz each)

125 g/4½ oz mayonnaise

a few drops of chilli sauce

125 g/4½ oz coconut pulp

½ tablespoon fresh coriander (cilantro) as garnish

black sesame seeds as garnish

❶ Wash the asparagus and remove the woody ends. Cut the asparagus stalks (stems) into pieces 7 cm/2¾ in long. Heat 2 tablespoons groundnut oil and fry the asparagus in it. Season with salt, pepper, 1 scant tablespoon Oriental mixed herbs and 2 scant tablespoons sesame oil.

❷ Wash the rabbit fillets, wipe dry, season with salt and pepper and fry in the remaining oil.

❸ Add the chilli sauce, a small amount of Oriental mixed herbs, a few drops of sesame oil and coconut pulp to the mayonnaise and stir to make a smooth mixture.

❹ Put some mayonnaise on four plates and arrange the asparagus and rabbit fillet on top. Garnish with coriander (cilantro) and sesame seeds.

Serves 4. About 724 kcal per serving

Asparagus, beans and meat gratin

This is a perfect dish when you have guests: it can be prepared the previous day and cooked in the oven for two hours so that it is ready for when your guests arrive.

1 kg/2¼ lb white asparagus

salt

1 pinch sugar

25 g/1 oz (2 tablespoons) butter

500 g/18 oz green (snap) beans

150 g/5½ oz mushrooms

1 onion

freshly ground pepper

200 g/7 oz streaky bacon

800 g/1¾ lb pork

450 ml/16 fl oz (2 cups) cream

150 g/5½ oz soft cream cheese

❶ Peel the asparagus, remove the woody ends and cook in boiling salted water with sugar and 1 teaspoon butter for 10 minutes until done. Remove from the water and drain.

❷ Wash the green (snap) beans, top and tail them and cut into pieces 2 cm/1¼ in long. Cook in boiling salted water until done. Take out of the water and drain.

❸ Wash the mushrooms, cut off the ends and cut into slices, not too thin. Peel the onion, chop coarsely. Sweat the onion and mushrooms in 1 tablespoon of butter until the onions are golden yellow. Season with salt and pepper and remove from the pan.

❹ Dice the bacon and fry in the remaining butter. Cut the meat into cubes, add to the bacon and fry. Season with salt and pepper. Put the meat and bacon in a gratin dish. Stir the vegetables and put on top of the meat.

❺ Heat the cream and melt the cheese in it. Pour the sauce over the vegetables. Cover the dish with aluminium foil and stand in the refrigerator for 24 hours.

❻ Pre-heat the oven to 200°C (400°F), Gas mark 6. Cook for 1 hour with the foil on top and another hour without the foil.

Serves 4. About 1,277 kcal per serving

Gratin of asparagus with smoked loin of pork

Loin of pork can be bought cooked or uncooked. For this particular dish, cooked loin is better. If necessary it can be ordered from the butcher.

1 kg/2¼ lb white asparagus

salt

1 pinch sugar

25 g/1 oz (2 tablespoons) butter

600 g/1¼ lb potatoes

butter for greasing the mould

250 g/9 oz smoked loin of pork, in slices

25 g/1 oz (4 tablespoons) flour

250 ml/8 fl oz (1 cup) white wine

150 g/5½ oz soft cream cheese

200 g/7 oz crème fraîche

freshly ground pepper

50 g/2 oz (½ cup) raclette cheese, grated

❶ Peel the asparagus, remove the woody ends and cut into pieces about 2.5 cm/1 in long. Cook in boiling water with sugar and 1 tablespoon butter for 10–5 minutes until done. Remove from the water and drain.

❷ Wash the potatoes, boil, drain and cut into slices. Arrange in a greased gratin dish. Put rolled slices of loin of pork and asparagus pieces on top.

❸ Warm the remaining butter, stir in the flour, add 250 ml/8 fl oz (1 cup) asparagus stock (broth) and wine, stirring constantly, and simmer for 5 minutes. Add the crème fraîche and cream cheese, season with salt and pepper and pour over the gratin.

❹ Sprinkle the grated cheese over the sauce and bake for 25–30 minutes in the oven pre-heated to 200°C (400°F), Gas mark 6.

Serves 4. About 647 kcal per serving

Veal medallions
with asparagus

Medallions of veal are among the most delicious and tender cuts of meat.

❶ Peel the white asparagus, wash the green asparagus and remove the woody ends. Cook the white asparagus for 15 minutes and the green asparagus for 10 minutes in gently simmering salted water with sugar and lemon juice.

❷ Season the veal medallions with salt and pepper and fry in clarified butter for 3 minutes on each side. Remove from the pan and keep in a warm place.

❸ Deglaze the cooking juices with wine. Stir in the flour and meat stock (broth), stirring constantly, and reduce a little. Add the cream and season with salt and pepper.

❹ Remove the asparagus from the stock (broth), drain and toss in hot butter.

Serves 4. About 479 kcal per serving

500 g/18 oz white asparagus

750 g/1½ lb green asparagus

salt

1 teaspoon sugar

juice of ½ lemon

**8 medallions of veal
   (about 80 g/3 oz each)**

freshly ground pepper

**20 g/¾ oz (1½ tablespoons)
   clarified butter**

**100 ml/3½ oz (scant ½ cup) dry
   white wine**

2 tablespoons wheat flour

**100 ml/3½ oz (scant ½ cup) meat
   stock (broth)**

100 ml/3½ oz (scant ½ cup) cream

20 g/¾ oz (1½ tablespoons) butter

Pork medallions with asparagus and dill

It is advisable to order the medallions from your butcher because they are not always easy to find. They are much sought after because of their very tender texture.

1 Peel and chop the onions. Peel the asparagus, remove the woody ends and cut into pieces 1 cm/⅜ in long. Wash the dill, dab it dry and chop finely. Rinse the medallions in cold water and season with salt and pepper.

2 Heat 80 g/3 oz (6 tablespoons) butter and oil in a pan and fry the meat for 2–3 minutes on both sides. Remove from the pan and keep warm in the oven at the lowest setting, 80°C (180°F).

3 Sweat the onion and asparagus in the cooking fat, add the veal stock (broth) and lemon juice and simmer for 7 minutes. Stir the remaining butter, bit by bit, into the sauce. Reduce a little and stir in the dill.

4 Arrange the medallions on the plates, pour the asparagus sauce on top and garnish with crab.

Serves 4. About 920 kcal per serving

4 onions

800 g/1¾ lb white asparagus

2 bunches dill

12 pork medallions
(about 800 g/1¾ lb in all)

salt

freshly ground pepper

250 g/9 oz (1¼ cups) ice-cold
butter

4 tablespoons oil

600 ml/1 pint (2½ cups) veal stock
(broth)

4 tablespoons lemon juice

100 g/3½ oz crab meat

Asparagus roulade

This dish can also be made with thin slices of chicken or turkey breast instead of veal.

1 Wash the asparagus, remove the woody ends and cut each piece of asparagus to half its length. Cook in gently simmering salted water with sugar and butter for 5 minutes until done. Remove from the water and drain.

2 Rinse the meat in cold water and wipe dry. Flatten with a tenderizing mallet. Put some curd cheese on each slice of veal, sprinkle with parsley and season with salt and pepper. Put the asparagus halves on top and roll up the veal slices. Coat the veal roulades in flour and secure with cocktail sticks.

3 Fry the roulades in oil, add a little asparagus stock (broth) and wine, cover and cook for about 20 minutes. Season the sauce to taste and reduce a little to thicken.

Serves 4. About 277 kcal per serving

8 thin, green asparagus sticks
(about 250 g/9 oz)

salt

½ teaspoon sugar

1 teaspoon butter

4 veal olives
(about 100 g/3½ oz each)

100 g/3½ oz curd cheese

1 bunch parsley

freshly ground pepper

1 tablespoon flour

1 tablespoon olive oil

125 ml/4 fl oz (½ cup) white wine

Asparagus with fillet of beef

This light but spicy dish uses fresh chilli pods. Remember that it is best to handle chillies under running water or to wear kitchen gloves.

4 pineapple slices with juice

750 g/1½ lb green asparagus

250 g/9 oz spring onions (scallions)

1 red chilli pod

salt

1 teaspoon sugar

10 g/⅜ oz (2 teaspoons) butter

400 g/14 oz fillet of beef

4 tablespoons oil

freshly ground pepper

3 tablespoons sherry

❶ Drain the pineapple slices, reserve the juice and cut each slice into four. Wash the asparagus, remove the woody ends and cut the asparagus stalks (stems) into pieces 2 cm/¾ in long. Wash and prepare the spring onions (scallions) and chop coarsely. Cut the chilli pods into half, remove the stalk, the white pith inside and seeds and cut into fine strips.

❷ Cook the asparagus in gently simmering water with sugar and butter for about 5 minutes. Remove from the water and drain.

❸ Rinse the beef fillet in cold water, wipe dry and slice into pieces 2–3 cm/¾–1¼ in thick. Fry quickly in hot oil over high heat. Season with salt and pepper and remove from the pan.

❹ Fry the spring onions (scallions). Add the asparagus, pineapple and chilli. Stir in 100 ml/3½ fl oz (scant ½ cup) pineapple juice and sherry and simmer for 3 minutes. Add the meat and season with salt and pepper. Serve with the asparagus.

Serves 4. About 333 kcal per serving

Duck with orange and asparagus

Duck à l'orange has become a classic combination. With asparagus, it becomes something even more special.

1 Heat the clarified butter and fry the duck breasts in it for 3 minutes on each side. Wrap each duck breast separately in aluminium foil and cook for 20 minutes in the oven pre-heated to 140°C (275°F), Gas mark 1.

2 Peel the asparagus, remove the woody ends and cook the asparagus in boiling salted water with 1 pinch of sugar and 20 g/¾ oz (1½ tablespoons) butter until tender.

3 Heat 20 g/¾ oz (1½ tablespoons) butter in a pan. Add 2 tablespoons sugar and caramelize, stirring constantly. Add the vinegar, veal stock (broth), orange juice and lemon juice. Stir in the finely grated orange and lemon zest. Bring to the boil and reduce the amount of liquid by half. Stir 60 g/2 oz (4 tablespoons) cold butter and season with salt and pepper.

4 Remove the duck breasts from the foil and stir the cooking juices into the sauce. Brush the duck breasts with this sauce and put them on the foil, skin side up. Brown under the grill until crisp.

5 Remove the duck breast from under the grill and cut into slices. Remove the asparagus from the water, drain and serve with the orange and lemon sauce.

Serves 4. About 508 kcal per serving

15 g/½ oz (1 tablespoon) clarified butter

4 duck breasts

1 kg/2¼ lb white asparagus

salt

sugar

100 g/3½ oz (½ cup) butter

125 ml/4 fl oz (½ cup) wine vinegar

100 ml/3½ oz (scant ½ cup) meat stock (broth)

juice and zest of 3 untreated oranges

juice and zest of 3 untreated lemons

freshly ground pepper

Peppered beef fillet with asparagus

You can also use another meat in this recipe. Instead of 4 large beef fillets, you could have 4 small beef fillets and four small pork fillets (tenderloin).

2 kg/4½ lb white asparagus

salt

15 g/½ oz (1 tablespoon) butter

650 g/1½ lb sliced beef fillet

freshly ground pepper

15 g/½ oz (1 tablespoon) clarified butter

250 g/9 oz (1¼ cups) butter

yolks of 4 eggs

2 tablespoons medium dry white wine

2 tablespoons parsley

lemon juice

❶ Peel the asparagus, remove the woody ends and cook in boiling water with 1 tablespoon butter for 10 minutes until tender.

❷ Season the slices of beef fillet generously with salt and coarsely ground pepper from the mill. Fry on both sides in the clarified butter.

❸ Melt the butter, remove from the heat and let it cool down a little. Put the egg yolks in a bowl standing in a container filled with hot water and whisk vigorously, stir in the white wine and chopped parsley. Continue whisking until the mixture turns pale yellow and becomes foamy. Add the melted butter, first drop by drop, then stir in slowly until you obtain a smooth, creamy mixture. Season the sauce with salt, pepper and lemon juice.

❹ Remove the asparagus from the water and drain. Arrange on the plates with the meat and serve with the hollandaise sauce.

Serves 4. About 877 kcal per serving

Lamb fillets with green asparagus

Ginger and chilli add a spicy, exotic touch to this dish. It is extremely easy
and instead of the chilli you can also use chilli paste or sambal oelek.

❶ Wash the asparagus, remove the woody ends and cut the asparagus
stalks (stems) into pieces 5 cm/2 in long. Blanch the tomatoes in hot
water, peel, remove the seeds and cut into small cubes.

❷ Rinse the lamb fillets under the cold water tap, wipe dry and cut into
small pieces. Peel the shallots and the ginger. Chop both finely. Wash the
chillies, cut lengthways, remove the stalk, the white pith inside and the
seeds. Dice finely.

❸ Heat 2 tablespoons olive oil, fry the asparagus for 2-3 minutes, add
125 ml/4 fl oz (1 cup) water, cover and cook for 10 minutes until tender.
Remove from the heat and stir in the tomatoes and chillies. Leave to
stand for a while.

❹ Heat the remaining oil and fry the lamb fillets for 5 minutes on each
side. Add the chopped shallots and ginger and fry briefly. Add the wine.
Add the asparagus to the meat. Season with salt and pepper and reduce
a little to thicken the sauce.

Serves 4. About 340 kcal per serving

1 kg/2¼ lb green asparagus

4 tomatoes

4 lamb fillets
(about 100 g/3½ oz each)

2 shallots

1 small piece fresh ginger
(about 1 cm/⅜ in)

2 small chillies

4 tablespoons olive oil

125 ml/4 fl oz (½ cup) dry white
wine

salt

freshly ground pepper

Beef fillets with asparagus in cream sauce

Button mushrooms are a little tastier than the larger, open mushrooms, but either kind can be used.

1 kg/2¼ lb white asparagus

salt

1 pinch sugar

15 g/½ oz (2 tablespoons) butter

1 tablespoon flour

2 tablespoons cream

freshly ground white pepper

1 tablespoon chopped parsley

1 spring onion (scallion)

125 g/4½ oz button mushrooms

1 tomato

4 slices fillet of beef
(about 100 g/3½ oz each)

1 teaspoon clarified butter

❶ Peel the asparagus and remove the woody ends. Cut the asparagus stalks (stems) into pieces 3 cm/1¼ in long and cook in boiling, salted water with sugar and 1 teaspoon butter for 10 minutes until tender. Remove from the water and drain over another saucepan.

❷ Heat 1 tablespoon butter, stir in the flour, add some asparagus stock (broth), stirring constantly, and reduce. Stir in the cream and season with salt and pepper. Add the asparagus and chopped parsley to the sauce and simmer over low heat.

❸ Wash the spring onion (scallion), peel and cut small. Wash and prepare the button mushrooms and cut into four. Blanch the tomatoes, peel, remove the seeds and chop coarsely. Sweat the onion, button mushrooms and tomatoes in the rest of the butter. Season with salt and pepper.

❹ Rinse the beef fillets and wipe dry. Season with salt and pepper and fry on both sides in the hot clarified butter. Arrange on plates together with the asparagus in cream sauce and the mushroom mixture. Serve immediately.

Serves 4. About 283 kcal per serving

150 g/5½ oz peas

2 spring onions (scallions)

60 g/2 oz (¼ cup) sugar

1 kg/2¼ lb white asparagus

25 g/1 oz (2 tablespoons) butter

salt

1 pinch sugar

400 g/14 oz chicken breast fillets

1 tablespoon curry powder

1 tablespoon flour

200 ml/7 fl oz (⅞ cup) chicken stock (broth), made from a cube

4 tablespoons cream

20 g/¾ oz capers with liquid

1 tablespoon lemon juice

freshly ground white pepper

4 large puff pastry vol-au-vent cases

Asparagus and chicken breast vol-au-vents

Many bakers sell ready-made vol-au-vent cases which are ideal for this recipe. If you cannot find any, they are easy to make from frozen puff pastry.

❶ Wash and prepare the peas and spring onions (scallions). Cut the spring onions (scallions) into rings. Wash the peas. Peel the asparagus, remove the woody ends and cut into small pieces.

❷ Melt the butter and fry the onions, peas and asparagus for 5 minutes. Season with salt and pepper. Cut the chicken into cubes, add to the pan and fry lightly. Sprinkle curry powder and flour over the meat and other ingredients and stir well. Next add the chicken stock (broth) and cream, stirring constantly. Cover and simmer for 5 minutes. Stir in the peas and capers with their juice. Season with lemon juice and pepper. Simmer gently for another 5 minutes.

❸ Arrange the vol-au-vents on the plates and fill with the asparagus and chicken mixture.

Serves 4. About 518 kcal per serving

Veal schnitzel in an egg-based coating with asparagus salad

The salad can be prepared some hours before the meal. This enables its full flavour to develop.

❶ Peel the white asparagus, wash the green asparagus and remove the woody ends. Cut the asparagus into pieces 3 cm/1¼ in long. Cook the white asparagus for about 15 minutes and the green asparagus for 8 minutes in gently simmering water with butter until tender. Remove from the water and drain.

❷ Chop the onion finely and add to the herbs, fruit vinegar, white wine, oil flavoured with herbs and mustard. Mix well and stir to make a smooth marinade. Season with salt and pepper. Stir gently into the asparagus.

❸ Beat the eggs. Rinse the veal schnitzel in cold water and wipe dry. Season with salt and pepper. Coat the escalopes in flour, dip in the beaten egg and fry immediately in the hot clarified butter.

Serves 4. About 587 kcal per serving

1 kg/2¼ lb white asparagus

1 kg/2¼ lb green asparagus

salt

15 g/½ oz (1 tablespoon) butter

½ red onion

1 tablespoon dill, finely chopped

1 tablespoon chives, finely chopped

1 tablespoon parsley, finely chopped

8 tablespoons strawberry vinegar

8 tablespoons dry white wine

6 tablespoons herb oil

2 teaspoons strong mustard

freshly ground pepper

4 eggs

8 small veal escalopes (about 80 g/3 oz each)

flour

25 g/1 oz (2 tablespoons) clarified butter

Fried asparagus with smoked loin of pork

The lightly smoked flavour of the meat goes very well with the asparagus.

❶ Peel the asparagus, remove the woody ends and cut diagonally into pieces 1 cm/⅜ in long. Peel and chop the shallots. Cut the meat into narrow strips. Blanch the tomatoes, peel, remove the stalks (stems) and chop coarsely.

❷ Fry the asparagus pieces briskly in 2 tablespoons groundnut oil, add the chopped shallots and fry with the asparagus. Add the chicken stock (broth) little by little and boil away to reduce the amount of liquid. Season with salt, pepper and soya sauce and simmer for a little longer.

❸ Fry the strips of pork in the rest of the oil. Arrange the asparagus on plates and serve with the strips of pork, chopped tomatoes and chervil.

Serves 4. About 211 kcal per serving

1.5 kg/3 lb white asparagus

2 shallots

300 g/11 oz smoked loin of pork,

2 tomatoes

4 tablespoons groundnut oil

200 ml/7 fl oz (⅞ cup) chicken stock (broth)

salt

freshly ground pepper

soya sauce

chervil as garnish

Asparagus with salted pork fillet (tenderloin)

Salted pork fillet (tenderloin) is not always available, so it is advisable to order it from the butcher in good time.

❶ Wash the asparagus and remove the woody ends. Wash the pork fillet (tenderloin), wipe dry and cook for 25 minutes in simmering water with 1 bay leaf and peppercorns.

❷ Cook the asparagus for 15–20 minutes in gently simmering water with a little sugar and butter.

❸ Purée the washed basil and parsley leaves with the eggs and creamed horseradish to make a creamy sauce.

❹ Remove the pork fillet (tenderloin) from the water and drain. Serve with the green sauce.

Serves 4. About 354 kcal per serving

1.5 kg/3 lb green asparagus

600 g/1¼ lb salted fillet of pork

1 bay leaf

8 peppercorns

salt

sugar

10 g/⅜ oz (2 teaspoons) butter

2 bunch parsley

2 bunch basil

3 peeled hard-boiled (hard-cooked) eggs

3 tablespoons creamed horseradish

Asparagus with veal quenelles in cream sauce

Depending on the size of quenelles you want, they can be made with either a teaspoon or a tablespoon.

2 kg/4½ lb white asparagus

salt

40 g/1½ oz (3 tablespoons) butter

600 g/1¼ lb minced (ground) veal

450 ml/16 fl oz (2 cups) cream

freshly ground white pepper

1 level tablespoon flour

1 bunch parsley

❶ Peel the asparagus, remove the woody ends and cut into pieces 3 cm/1¼ in long. Cook in boiling salted water with 1 tablespoon butter for 10 minutes until tender. Remove from the water and keep in a warm place. Stir 1 glass of cream into the minced (ground) veal to make a smooth mixture. Season with salt and pepper.

❷ Heat the remaining butter, stir in the flour and add a little asparagus stock (broth) to make a creamy sauce. Add the remaining cream and reduce the sauce a little to thicken it. Season with salt and pepper. Add the asparagus and three-quarters of the finely chopped parsley.

❸ Heat the asparagus stock (broth). Form the veal quenelles with a spoon and simmer very gently in the asparagus stock (broth) over a low heat. Arrange the asparagus on the plates with the veal quenelles around it. Pour the sauce on top garnish with the rest of the herbs.

Serves 4. About 680 kcal per serving

Turkey and asparagus fricassée

This excellent turkey, morel and asparagus fricassée is delicious served with rice or French bread.

20 g/¾ oz morels

1 bunch chives

500 g/18 oz white asparagus

1 bunch soup vegetables
   (parsley, carrots, celery, leeks)

600 g/1¼ lb turkey meat

30 g/1 oz (2 tablespoons) butter

1 tablespoon flour

225 ml/8 fl oz (1 cup) cream

freshly ground white pepper

salt

❶ Soak the morels for 1 hour in warm water. Take out and squeeze to remove as much water as possible. Wash the chives, dry and chop finely.

❷ Peel the asparagus, remove the woody ends and cut into small pieces. Cook in boiling salted water for 10 minutes until tender. Remove and drain.

❸ Wash and prepare the vegetables for the soup. Chop the vegetables and meat and fry them in the butter. Add 250 ml/8 fl oz (1 cup) asparagus stock (broth) and bring to the boil. Sprinkle with flour, stir and boil briefly to reduce.

❹ Add the morels and cook for 20 minutes over a low heat. Add the asparagus and stir in the cream. Season with salt and pepper. Garnish with chives.

Serves 4. About 332 kcal per serving

Asparagus and meatball stew

This dish is not only quick to prepare but because of its fine ingredients, it makes a delicious, light variation on the more traditional stews.

500 g/18 oz white asparagus

500 g/18 oz potatoes

30 g/1 oz (2 tablespoons) butter

salt

1 pinch sugar

300 g/11 oz frozen meat balls

300 g/11 oz frozen peas

125 ml/4 fl oz (½ cup) cream

yolks of 2 eggs

1 bunch smooth parsley

❶ Peel the asparagus, remove the woody ends and cut the asparagus into pieces 2 cm/1¼ in long. Boil the woody ends and peelings in 500 ml/17 fl oz (2¼ cups) water. Peel the potatoes, wash and cut into large cubes.

❷ Fry the asparagus and potatoes in butter. Pour the asparagus stock (broth) through a sieve and add to the potatoes and asparagus. Season with salt and sugar and simmer for 10 minutes.

❸ Add the deep-frozen meatballs and peas and cook for a further 10 minutes. Stir the egg yolk into the cream. Wash the parsley, dry, chop finely and sprinkle on the stew.

Serves 4. About 452 kcal per serving

Spaghettini with duck and asparagus sauce

Instead of red peppers, tomatoes, fresh corn on the cob or mushrooms such as chanterelles or button mushrooms can be used.

300 g/11 oz green asparagus

1 sweet red pepper

1 sweet green pepper

500 g/18 oz spaghettini

400 g/14 oz duck breast fillets

olive oil

For the sauce:

3 tablespoons lime juice

1 tablespoon medium strength mustard

2 tablespoons olive oil

1 tablespoon parsley

❶ Wash the asparagus, remove the woody ends and blanch the asparagus. Cut the peppers in four, removing the stalks (stems), seeds and white pith inside. Wash the cut paprika. Stir all the sauce ingredients together.

❷ Cook the spaghettini *al dente* in boiling salted water.

❸ Brush the duck fillets with olive oil and brown for 2–3 minutes under the grill. Sprinkle the asparagus and peppers with olive oil and grill (broil) together with the meat for a further 2 minutes. Take the duck breasts and peppers out of the oven and cut into strips.

❹ Arrange the spaghettini on plates, garnish with the strips of duck fillets and vegetables. Pour the sauce on top.

Serves 4. About 783 kcal per serving

400 g/14 oz veal

2 teaspoons cornflour (cornstarch)

salt

freshly ground pepper

125 ml/4 fl oz (½ cup) white wine

½ bunch chives

500 g/18 oz green asparagus

1 cup cream

1 pinch sugar

1 shallot

1 small piece fresh ginger (about 1 cm/⅜ in)

2 tablespoons olive oil

250 g/9 oz mixed vegetables

½ teaspoon paprika

Asparagus with veal in cream sauce

This light, exotic asparagus and veal dish is delicious served with white or green tagliatelle, rice or toasted slices of white bread.

❶ Rinse the meat under the cold water tap, wipe dry and cut into thin strips. Stir the cornflour (cornstarch), salt and pepper into 2 tablespoons white wine to make a smooth mixture. Dip the strips of meat into it. Wash the chives, dab dry and chop finely.

❷ Wash the asparagus, remove the woody ends and cut into pieces about 4 cm/1½ in long. Put the tips to one side. Add 125 ml/4 fl oz (1 cup) water to the cream and bring to the boil. Season with salt and sugar and cook the asparagus pieces in it for about 5 minutes. Add the asparagus tips and cook for a further 5 minutes.

❸ Peel the shallots and ginger, chop both finely and fry in olive oil until golden yellow. Add the meat and fry for 2–3 minutes. Add the rest of the wine. Add the mixed vegetables and simmer gently for a few minutes until the sauce becomes creamy.

❹ Add the asparagus in the cream sauce to the meat, season with salt, paprika and pepper and garnish with chives.

Serves 4. About 358 kcal per serving

Turkey fricassée with green asparagus

This dish is delicious served with rice, particularly wild rice.

800 g/1¾ lb green asparagus

salt

sugar

80 g/3 oz (6 teaspoons) butter

100 g/3½ oz button mushrooms, canned or preserved in a jar

400 g/14 oz turkey breast

2 tablespoons oil

225 ml/8 fl oz (1 cup) cream

200 g/7 oz mixed vegetable

freshly ground pepper

8 tablespoons breadcrumbs

❶ Wash the asparagus and remove the woody ends. Cook in gently simmering salted water with a pinch of sugar and 1 teaspoon butter for 15 minutes until tender.

❷ Take the button mushrooms out of the jar or can, drain and reserve 200 ml/7 fl oz (⅞ cup) of the liquid. Cut the turkey meat into strips, fry in hot oil and take out of the pan. Add the mushroom liquid and cream to the cooking juices and bring to the boil to reduce and thicken.

❸ Heat the meat, button mushrooms and mixed vegetables in the sauce and season with salt and pepper.

❹ Heat the rest of the butter and fry the breadcrumbs in it. Remove the asparagus from the water and drain. Arrange on a plate and sprinkle with the fried breadcrumbs.

Serves 4. About 508 kcal per serving

Fried asparagus with pork chops

Instead of chops you can also use escalopes which are often sold already cut small.

1.2 kg/2½ lb white asparagus

1 untreated lemon

600 g/1¼ lb pork chops without bones

3 tablespoons oil

5 tablespoons soya sauce

salt

freshly ground pepper

1 bunch chives

❶ Peel the asparagus and remove the woody ends. Cut the asparagus into pieces 4 cm/1½ in long. Rinse the lemons in hot water and wipe dry. Peel half the lemon thinly and cut the zest into thin strips.

❷ Cut the meat into thin strips, fry in hot oil, add the asparagus and fry for 3–4 minutes, stirring constantly. Add 2 tablespoons lemon juice and season with salt and pepper. Add the lemon zest and finely chopped chives.

Serves 4. About 325 kcal per serving

Sauces and dips

In all their variety, sauces provide an embarrassment of choice. Even variations on the same recipe give completely different nuances of tastes. For instance, the addition of different ingredients to the classic Hollandaise sauce (page 122) such as lime (page 124), walnuts (page 122), truffles (page 124) or basil (page 124) gives a range of distinct sauces. Other interesting sauces described here include Herb sauce (page 134) providing an aromatic alternative, the refreshing Lemon sauce (page 130), Tomato and basil sauce (page 136), and Tarragon sauce (page 134). The exquisite Orange foam sauce (page 131) and Avocado sauce (see page 132) will delight gourmets who will also be intrigued by the Bacon sauce (page 125) and Strawberry sauce (page 131).

Hollandaise sauce

The eggs must be taken out of the refrigerator at least 2 hours before using so that they are at room temperature.

yolks of 4 eggs
2 teaspoons lemon juice
salt
freshly ground white pepper
250 g/9 oz (1¼ cups) butter

Stir the egg yolks and lemon together, season with salt and pepper and whisk vigorously to obtain a creamy texture. Put in a bain-marie and stir over simmering water until it has thickened sufficiently. Add warm, melted butter little by little, whisking all the time.

Serves 4. About 535 kcal per serving

Walnut hollandaise sauce

This is a delicious and easy variation on hollandaise sauce, simply made by the addition of finely chopped walnuts.

ingredients for hollandaise sauce (see above)
In addition:
80 g/3 oz (6 tablespoons) butter
60 g/2½ oz (½ cup) walnuts

❶ Make hollandaise sauce as shown in the recipe above.

❷ Cut the butter into pieces and whisk into the sauce little by little. Chop the walnuts finely and stir into the sauce.

Serves 4. About 382 kcal per serving

Lime-flavoured hollandaise sauce

Limes have a much more intense flavour than lemons, so it well worth trying to find them for this sauce.

ingredients for hollandaise sauce (see page 122)

In addition:

1 untreated lime

freshly ground pepper

❶ Make hollandaise sauce as shown in the recipe on page 122.

❷ Wash the lime under running hot water, wipe dry and grate 1–2 teaspoons of zest. Stir into the hollandaise and season with pepper.

Serves 4. About 535 kcal per serving

Basil-flavoured hollandaise sauce

ingredients for hollandaise sauce (see page 122)

In addition:

1–2 tablespoons tomato purée

1 untreated lemon

fresh basil

❶ Make hollandaise sauce as shown in the recipe on page 122.

❷ Stir in the tomato purée. Wash the lemon under running hot water, wipe dry, grate the zest and add more or less according to taste.

❸ Wash the basil, dab dry, remove the leaves, cut into fine strips and add to the sauce.

Serves 4. About 540 kcal per serving

Truffle-based hollandaise sauce

ingredients for hollandaise sauce (see page 122)

In addition:

125 g/4½ oz (⅝ cup) truffle butter or some truffle oil

In the recipe for hollandaise sauce, page 122, replace half the butter – 125 g/4½ oz (⅝ cup) – with truffle butter.

Or:

Make hollandaise sauce as shown in the recipe on page 122 and add a few drops of truffle oil to the sauce.

Serves 4. About 540 kcal per serving

Bacon sauce

8 spring onions (scallions)

12 small tomatoes

4 small chillies

400 g/14 oz bacon

200 g/7 oz (1 cup) butter

Chilli gives this sauce a pleasantly spicy touch!

❶ Wash the spring onions (scallions), prepare and cut into fine rings. Wash the tomatoes and cut into four. Cut the chillies in half, remove the stalks (stems), the white pith inside and the seeds. Dice the bacon finely.

❷ Melt 80 g/3 oz (6 tablespoons) butter, add the bacon and spring onions (scallions) and fry lightly. Add the tomatoes and chillies and cook for another 5 minutes. Stir in the remaining butter.

Serves 4. About 1105 kcal per serving

Egg sauce

6 hard-boiled (hard-cooked) eggs

80 g/3 oz (6 tablespoons) butter

1 pinch powdered mustard

salt

freshly ground pepper

freshly grated nutmeg

1 tablespoon parsley, finely chopped

1 tablespoon chives, finely chopped

Asparagus arranged on a large serving dish, draped in egg sauce and garnished with chopped egg and herbs, is not only a delight to the palate but a pleasure to the eye.

❶ Cut the eggs in half, remove the egg yolks and mash. Melt the butter and stir in the mashed egg yolks. Season with mustard powder, salt, pepper and nutmeg.

❸ Finely chop the egg white. Stir in the parsley and chives. Season with salt and pepper.

Serves 4. About 267 kcal per serving

Olive and egg sauce

2 hard-boiled (hard-cooked) eggs

2 tablespoons black olives,
stoned (pitted)

1 tablespoon fresh herbs

1 teaspoon capers

1 sardine fillets

6 tablespoons olive oil

3 tablespoons white wine
vinegar

freshly ground white pepper

salt

The capers and anchovy give this sauce a spicy edge. It is delicious served with a refreshing light white wine.

❶ Shell the eggs and separate the whites from the yolks. Finely chop them, separately.

❷ Chop the olives, herbs, capers and anchovies very finely. Stir in the oil and vinegar. Add the chopped egg yolks and egg whites. Season with salt and pepper.

Serves 4. About 235 kcal per serving

Yoghurt and herb sauce

The garlic can easily be omitted from this deliciously refreshing sauce if you prefer it without.

Wash the herbs, dab dry and chop finely. Peel the shallots and chop finely. Peel and crush or press the garlic. Mix well and stir into a smooth sauce together with the other ingredients.

Serves 4. About 138 kcal per serving

6 tablespoons fresh herbs

2 small shallots

2 cloves garlic

3 cups full fat yoghurt

2 tablespoons olive oil

2 tablespoons balsamic vinegar

freshly ground pepper

salt

Sabayon

This recipe is an unsweetened version of the celebrated Italian dessert, zabaglione. It is an excellent accompaniment for asparagus. The white wine can be replaced by a similar amount of vegetable or meat stock (broth).

Put the egg yolks in a bowl, season with salt and pepper and whisk to obtain a homogenous mixture. Place the bowl in hot bain-marie, gradually stir in the white wine and whisk until foamy and the mixture has thickened a little. Season with salt, pepper, lemon juice and vermouth. Stir in the tarragon and parsley.

Serves 4. About 111 kcal per serving

yolks of 4 eggs

freshly ground pepper

salt

200 ml/7 fl oz (⅞ cup) dry white wine

1 teaspoon lemon juice

1 tablespoon dry vermouth

1 tablespoon chopped tarragon

1 tablespoon chopped parsley

Cheese sauce

This cheese sauce acquires an exquisite asparagus aroma if asparagus stock (broth) is used instead of water.

❶ Heat the water, make the sauce mix and bring to the boil. Melt the processed cheese in it and stir to obtain a smooth texture. Add the crème fraîche and season with salt, pepper and lemon juice.

❷ Mix the lemon zest and Parmesan. Sprinkle on the sauce when it is served.

Serves 4. About 450 kcal per serving

1 packet light sauce mix to make 250 ml/8 fl oz (1 cup) liquid

200 g/7 oz soft cream cheese

150 g/5½ oz crème fraîche

salt

freshly ground pepper

1 tablespoon lemon juice

1 tablespoon grated zest of 1 untreated lemon

5 tablespoons grated Parmesan

Paprika and yoghurt sauce

Quick and easy to prepare, this sauce adds an exotic note to any asparagus dish

Stir some cornflour (cornstarch) and paprika into a little cold stock (broth). Heat the remaining stock (broth) and cream, stir in the paprika mixture, bring to the boil and cook for 1–2 minutes, stirring constantly. Remove the sauce from the heat and stir in the yoghurt. Season with salt and pepper.

Serves 4. About 108 kcal per serving

3 teaspoons cornflour (cornstarch)

2 teaspoons paprika

200 ml/7 fl oz (⅞ cup) vegetable or chicken stock (broth)

100 ml/3½ oz (scant ½ cup) cream

150 g/5½ oz natural yoghurt

1 pinch salt

1 pinch sugar

Lemon sauce

1 onion

20 g/¾ oz (1½ tablespoons) butter

1 teaspoon cornflour (cornstarch)

250 g/9 oz mascarpone

juice and peel of 1 untreated
    lemon

salt

freshly ground pepper

1 pinch sugar

This lemon sauce can be garnished with lemon balm and thin slices of lemon just before serving.

❶ Peel the onions, chop them coarsely and sweat in the butter. Add 500 ml/17 fl oz (2¼ cups) water or asparagus stock (broth) and bring to the boil, reducing the liquid to about half.

❷ Stir in the cornflour (cornstarch) and bring to the boil again. Stir in the mascarpone, lemon zest and lemon juice little by little. Heat again but do not boil. Season with salt, pepper and 1 pinch of sugar.

Serves 4. About 313 kcal per serving

Quark sauce

1 small onion

60 g/2 oz (4 tablespoons) butter

50 ml/1½ fl oz (5 tablespoons)
    dry white wine

50 ml/1½ fl oz (5 tablespoons)
    white wine-vinegar

100 g/3½ oz low fat curd cheese

100 ml/3½ oz (scant ½ cup) milk

1 tablespoon tarragon leaves,
    chopped

salt

freshly ground pepper

Worcestershire sauce

This quark sauce can also be made using soya or Cumberland sauce instead of Worcestershire sauce.

❶ Peel the onions, chop finely and sweat in 30 g/1 oz (2 tablespoons) butter until transparent. Add the wine and vinegar and reduce the liquid to about one-third. Add the remaining butter and stir to incorporate it. Allow to cool down.

❷ Mix the quark and milk and stir until smooth. Stir in the tarragon. Season the sauce with salt, pepper and Worcestershire sauce.

Serves 4. About 165 kcal per serving

Strawberry sauce

Do not liquidize all the strawberries but put a few aside so that you can garnish each plate of asparagus with a few strawberries.

❶ Wash the strawberries, hull them and cut into small pieces. Peel the onions, chop finely and sweat in the butter until transparent. Add half the strawberries, cook and liquidize.

❷ Stir the soured cream, almond flakes and honey into the sauce. Heat again but do not bring to the boil. Season with salt, pepper and ginger. Add the remaining strawberries just before serving.

Serves 4. About 187 kcal per serving

250 g/9 oz strawberries
2 small onions
1 teaspoon butter
150 ml/5 fl oz (⅝ cup) sour cream
2 tablespoons almond flakes
1 tablespoon honey
salt
freshly ground pepper
ginger, ground

Orange foam sauce

The sauce can also be ganrnished with a few thin slices of orange just before serving.

❶ Wash the orange in hot water, wipe dry, grate the zest and squeeze the juice. Separate the egg whites and yolks and reserve one egg white in a cup.

❷ Whisk the egg yolks with the orange juice in a bain-marie, until the mixture turns foamy. Stir in the crème fraîche and orange zest.

❸ Add a pinch of salt to the egg white and whisk until it forms stiff peaks, fold into the sauce and garnish with chervil.

Serves 4. About 211 kcal per serving

1 untreated orange
3 eggs
150 g/5½ oz crème fraîche
salt
chervil as garnish

Green sauce

200 g/7 oz creamed spinach, frozen

2 onions

25 g/1 oz (2 tablespoons) butter

200 g/7 oz crème fraîche

salt

freshly ground pepper

Green sauce made from spinach and cream is particularly good with asparagus and small new potatoes, tossed in butter.

❶ Defrost the spinach, peel the onions and chop finely.

❷ Melt the butter, add the onions and fry until transparent. Add the spinach and cook. Stir in the crème fraîche. Season with salt and pepper.

Serves 4. About 300 kcal per serving

Avocado sauce

125 ml/4 fl oz (½ cup) milk

1 small container hollandaise sauce of about 60 ml/2 fl oz (6 tablespoons)

2 avocados

juice of 1 lemon

1 pinch sugar

freshly ground pepper

Naturally avocado sauce can also be made with home-made hollandaise. For the hollandaise sauce, see recipe p. 122

❶ Heat up the milk with 150 ml/5 fl oz (⅝ cup) asparagus stock (broth), stir in the hollandaise sauce and bring to the boil.

❷ Halve the avocados, remove the stones (seeds) and scoop out the pulp with a spoon, mash and sprinkle with lemon juice

❸ Stir the avocado purée into the hollandaise sauce and season with sugar and pepper.

Serves 4. About 275 kcal per serving

Herb sauce

1 teaspoon mustard

125 g/4½ oz low fat milk yoghurt

1 tablespoon lemon juice

salt

freshly ground pepper

2 tablespoons chopped herbs:
parsley, chives, chervil, dill,
green coriander (cilantro)

100 ml/3½ oz (scant ½ cup) cream

The herbs used to flavour this sauce can be varied according to taste or depending on what is available in your herb garden.

❶ Stir the mustard, yoghurt and lemon juice together to make a smooth sauce. Season with salt and pepper and add the herbs.

❷ Whip the cream until thick and stir into the herb sauce.

Serves 4. About 78 kcal per serving

Tarragon sauce

2 eggs

juice of 1 lemon

450 ml/16 fl oz (2 cups) cream

4 teaspoons mustard, medium
strong

4 tablespoons tarragon vinegar

2 bunches tarragon

olive oil

salt

freshly ground pepper

The appearance and taste of this sauce can be altered by adding 2–3 peeled, chopped tomatoes to it.

Stir the eggs, lemon, cream, mustard and tarragon vinegar together. Add the finely chopped tarragon and olive oil. Season with salt and pepper.

Serves 4. About 350 kcal per serving

White wine sauce

50 ml/1½ fl oz (5 tablespoons) dry, medium white wine

2 tablespoons mustard, medium strong

6 tablespoons mayonnaise

salt

cayenne pepper

Cayenne pepper gives this sauce a rather spicy taste. For a milder sauce, replace the cayenne with white pepper.

Mix together wine, mustard and mayonnaise and stir until you obtain mixture. Season with salt and cayenne pepper.

Serves 4. About 732 kcal per serving

Tomato and basil sauce

6 tomatoes

2 bunch basil

3 shallots

15 g/½ oz (1 tablespoon) butter

6 teaspoons sherry or white wine vinegar

60 ml/2 fl oz (6 tablespoons) oil

375 ml/13 fl oz (generous 1½ cups) white wine

3 tablespoons lemon juice

salt

freshly ground pepper

This tomato and basil sauce can be served hot or cold with asparagus. It is excellent accompanied by crusty French bread.

❶ Wash the tomatoes and cut in half. Chop the flesh finely. Wash the basil, dab dry and cut the leaves into thin strips.

❷ Peel the shallots, dice finely and fry them in butter. Stir in the vinegar, oil, white wine and lemon juice. Bring to the boil and reduce the liquid to two-thirds. Stir the tomatoes and basil into the sauce and season with salt and pepper.

Serves 4. About 260 kcal per serving

Cheese dip

Stir all the ingredients together and season with the condiments listed.

Serves 4. About 324 kcal per serving

200 g/7 oz cream curd cheese

225 ml/8 fl oz (1 cup) cream

salt

freshly ground pepper

1 teaspoon parsley, finely chopped

1 teaspoon chervil, finely chopped

1 teaspoon lemon balm, finely chopped

Orange dip

Stir all the ingredients together and season with the condiments listed.

Serves 4. About 100 kcal per serving

125 ml/4 fl oz (½ cup) double (heavy) cream, whipped

3 tablespoons orange juice

½ teaspoon sugar

1 pinch salt

ginger, ground

Tomato dip

Stir all the ingredients together and season with the condiments listed.

Serves 4. About 64 kcal per serving

70 g//2½ oz tomato purée

3 tablespoons crème fraîche

juice of ½ lemon

salt

freshly ground pepper

1 pinch sugar

Cooking glossary

Glossary of technical and foreign language cooking terms

baking, roasting

Cooking food in the oven in a heat-resistant dish, in a baking tin (pan) or on a baking (cookie) sheet. The food is cooked by the hot air of a conventional or a fan oven (in a fan oven the same cooking effect is achieved with a lower temperature; see the maker's manual). The temperature most commonly used is 180°C (350°F), Gas Mark 4, which is ideal for cakes, biscuits (cookies), tarts, flans, roasts, fish and poultry. For puff pastry, soufflés and gratins the temperature should be between 200°C (400°F), Gas mark 6 and 220°C (425°F), Gas mark 7. More delicate food such as fish, veal and some poultry may need a lower heat, from 150°C (300°F), Gas mark 2 to 160°C (325°F), Gas mark 3.

As a rule of thumb, the lower the temperature, the longer the cooking time.

bain-marie

A container of hot water in which or over which food is gently cooked. It may be a rectangular pan in which pans are placed, but in the domestic kitchen it usually takes the form of a double boiler, a saucepan with a smaller pan fitting over it. It can be improvised satisfactorily by using a bowl over a saucepan containing about 2.5 cm/1 inch of hot water.

A bain-marie is used when it is essential not to overheat what is being cooked. It is used for processes such as melting chocolate, and for cooking sauces or puddings containing cream or eggs. For instance, to make a chocolate mousse, the egg whites are beaten stiff over a warm bain-marie. This makes a particularly airy, light yet firm mousse. A bain-marie is also indispensable for making a successful Hollandaise or Béarnaise sauce. The egg yolks are slowly heated while being stirred until they reach the correct consistency, so that they combine with the melted butter whisked into it little by little.

barding

Covering very lean meat such as saddle of venison, pheasant or saddle of hare with slices of bacon, secured with kitchen string. This ensures that the meat remains juicy and does not dry out, while also adding a pleasant flavour to the meat.

basting

Spooning liquid over food while it is being roasted. Normally the cooking juices are used, but butter, wine, stock (broth) or plain water can be used as well. This constant basting and 'looking after' the meat ensures that it remains juicy and does not dry out. The basting liquid acquires a very intense flavour.

beurre manié

Kneaded butter, used to thicken casseroles

and sauces. Equal amounts of flour and butter are kneaded together and added as small knobs into boiling liquid while stirring constantly. This thickening agent has a delicious buttery taste and it is easy to handle because the butter and flour are mixed before being adding to the liquid, reducing the risk of lumps forming in the course of cooking.

blanching

Cooking vegetables such as spinach, leeks and carrots briefly in fast-boiling water. It is important to refresh the vegetables by plunging them in ice-cold water immediately afterwards. This ensures that the vegetables remain crisp and retain their original colour. After blanching, the vegetables are heated in hot stock (broth) or butter before serving.

blini

Pancake (crepe) made of a Russian batter using buckwheat flour, fried in a special small frying pan (skillet) about 15 cm (6 in) in diameter. Wheat flour is often added to the buckwheat flour so that it binds more easily. Blinis are usually served with caviar. They are also delicious with braised meat and game.

boiling

Cooking in liquid that is boiling. The process is synonymous with the concept of cooking. The food is cooked in a large amount of water and the agitation of the liquid will prevent the ingredients sticking to each other. So long as the water is boiling, the temperature will be 100°C (212°F) for the whole of the cooking time.

bouquet garni

A small bundle of various fresh herbs (usually parsley, thyme and bay leaves), tied together and cooked with the food. The bouquet garni is removed before serving.

braising

This refers to a method of cooking which combines frying, simmering and steaming. First the food is seared in hot oil or fat on all sides. This seals the meat, forming a thin crust; this also forms roasting matter on the bottom of the pan which is very important for the colour and flavour of the sauce. Liquid is then added to the meat, the pan is sealed with a lid and the food is slowly braised in a preheated oven. The method is also good for vegetable and fish dishes. It is excellent for less tender, strongly flavoured cuts of meat such as oxtail, goulash, braising steak or stewing lamb.

breadcrumbs

Dried white crumbs, made from stale bread without the crust. They are used in stuffing mixtures or to coat fish, poultry or other meats such as lamb chops.

brunoise

Finely diced vegetables or potatoes.

canapé

Small, bite-sized pieces of bread with various toppings such as smoked salmon, foie gras, caviar, smoked duck breast, ham and so on. They are served as an appetizer.

carcass

The carcass of poultry used in the preparation of chicken stock (broth). Fish bones are used in a similar way to make fish stock (broth).

carving

Cutting meat or poultry into slices or small pieces for serving. It is a good idea to carve on a carving board with a groove for the juices, using a special carving knife.

casserole

A large heat-resistant cooking pot usually made of cast iron or earthenware, excellent for slow-cooked dishes, braises and stews such as oxtail and game ragout. Because of the casserole's large surface area and the lengthy cooking time, the meat is able to release its full flavour. Casseroles may be round or oval, the latter shape being ideally suited for long-shaped pieces of meat such as leg of lamb, rolled cuts of meat or a chicken.

célestine

Fine strips of pancake (crepe) added to soup as a garnish.

chiffonade

Finely cut strips of lettuce, often served with shrimp cocktail.

chinois

Conical strainer or sieve used to strain sauces and soups.

clarification

The removal of cloudy matter from soups, stock (broth) or jelly with lightly beaten egg white. The egg white attracts all the foreign particles which cause the cloudiness and they can then be easily removed. The operation is carried out as follows. A lightly beaten egg white is added to some lean minced (ground) beef and chopped vegetables and a few ice cubes are stirred in. The mixture is added to the stock (broth), which should also be well chilled. Heat up while stirring constantly. The egg white begins to thicken at 70°C (160°F) and in the process it attracts all the impurities in the stock (broth). The stock (broth) becomes clear while developing a very intense flavour, as a result of the beef and vegetables. Fish and vegetable stock (broth) can also be clarified in the same way; in these cases the meat is omitted.

coating

The operation of pouring sauce over vegetables, meat or fish.

It also describes the technique of covering slices of meat and fish with beaten egg and breadcrumbs before frying them in hot oil. This gives the food a crisp coating while keeping the inside moist and juicy.

concassée

Blanched, peeled, quartered and de-seeded tomatoes, finely chopped. The term may also be applied to herbs.

consommé

Simple soup made of meat or chicken stock (broth), sometimes garnished. When clarified, it is known as clear or "double" consommé. Cold consommé is often a jelly.

cream soup, velouté soup

Cream soups are thickened with béchamel sauce. Velouté soups are thickened with an egg and cream mixture. The soup should not be brought back to the boil after the mixture has been added because the egg yolk would curdle.

crepes

Thin pancakes made from a batter consisting of milk, flour and eggs. The pancakes are cooked slowly in a frying pan (skillet) until golden. They can be served as a dessert, plain with a sprinkling of sugar and lemon juice, or spread or filled with jam or chocolate. They can also be served as a savoury dish, stuffed with vegetable or other fillings.

deep-frying

The process of cooking food by immersion in hot fat. When the food is cooked and crisp, it is removed from the fat or oil in its basket or with a skimming ladle and left to drain thoroughly on kitchen paper. Because hot oil or fat often spatters it is vital to be extremely careful and avoid the risk of fire. An electric chip pan with an adjustable thermostatically controlled temperature control is an excellent idea not only because it is safer but it also creates much less of a smell. Peeled potatoes cut into chips (sticks) or slices, shrimps and vegetables in batter are ideal for deep-frying, while deep-fried semolina dumplings are delicious served in soup. Deep-frying is also used for sweet dishes such as doughnuts and apple fritters.

duxelles

Garnish or stuffing consisting of finely chopped mushrooms sweated with diced onions and herbs.

forcemeat or stuffing

Finely chopped meat or fish used to stuff eggs, meat, pasta and so on. It can make a dish in its own right, as in the case of meat balls and quenelles, for example. It is also used as a basis for terrines and pâtés such as deer terrine or wild boar pâté.

filleting

The operation of cutting off the undercut of beef sirloin or similar cuts of pork (tenderloin), veal or lamb; removing the breasts of poultry from the carcass; or cutting the flesh of fish in strip-like pieces from the backbone.

flambé

Pouring spirits (such as brandy, rum or Grand Marnier) over food and setting light to it. The process is used with both savoury and sweet dishes, such as Crêpes Suzette. The spirits need to be warmed slightly first.

fleurons

Small pieces of puff pastry baked into various shapes such as flowers, little ships or shrimps. They are served with fish dishes in a sauce or with chicken fricassée.

flouring

The coating of pieces of fish or meat with flour before frying. This forms a tasty crust round the meat or fish which will be particularly juicy as a result.

frying

Frying is the process of cooking food in hot fat. The best fats and oils for frying are therefore ones that can be heated to a high temperature such as sunflower oil, clarified butter or goose fat. When butter is used, a little oil is often added to raise the temperature it will reach without burning. Some cuts of meat such as beef steaks or pork cutlets may be fried in a non-stick griddle pan without any fat.

gazpacho

Cold Spanish vegetable soup made with fresh tomatoes, cucumbers, garlic and fresh herbs. It is particularly delicious on a hot summer's day.

glazing

Creating a glossy surface on vegetables, meat, fish or puddings. A suitable stock (broth), the cooking juices, a light caramel, jelly, hot jam or icing is poured over the food in question.

gnocchi

Small dumplings, originally Italian, made from potato, semolina or bread flour, depending on the region, poached briefly in boiling water.

gratiné

Baking dishes under a very high top heat until a brown crust has formed. The ideal topping is grated cheese, breadcrumbs or a mixture of the two.

grilling (broiling)

Cooking with intense radiant heat, provided by gas, electricity or charcoal, the latter giving the food a particularly delicious flavour. The food is cooked on a grid without fat, and grilling (broiling) is therefore particularly good for people who are calorie conscious. Meat, fish, poultry and even vegetables can be cooked in this way.

healthy eating

A well-balanced, varied diet based on wholesome, nutritious foods in the right proportion. Ingredients recommended include wholemeal (wholewheat) products, organic meat, fish and poultry and fresh fruit and vegetables.

julienne

Peeled vegetables cut into thin sticks, the length and thickness of matchsticks. They are cooked in butter or blanched and used as a garnish for soup, fish, meat or poultry dishes.

jus

The name given to cooking juices produced during roasting. It is also used to describe brown stock (broth) prepared from various kinds of meat.

kaltschale

Literally "cold cup", this is a cold sweet soup made with fruit and wine. The fruit, for instance raspberries, melon and strawberries, is finely puréed with lemon juice and wine if so desired to which fresh herbs are added. It is important that it is served chilled.

larding needle

Special needle for pulling lardons (strips of pork fat) through lean meat to keep it moist and make it more tender.

marinade

A mixture based on vinegar, lemon juice, buttermilk or yoghurt, with onions and other vegetables, spices and herbs. Meat or fish is steeped in the mixture for several hours to make it tender and enhance its flavour. Marinades can also be used for dressing salads or for marinating meat that is already tender. Meat marinades give sauces a particularly delicious flavour because they have absorbed the various flavours from the herbs, vegetables and spices.

marinating

Steeping meat or fish in a liquid containing salt, wine, vinegar, lemon juice or milk, and flavourings such as herbs and spices. Marinating has a tenderizing effect on the food and also improves the flavour because of the various ingredients added to the marinade. In addition, marinating also has a preserving effect on meat or fish so that it keeps longer. For instance, raw salmon may be marinated in salt, sugar, herbs and spices.

minestrone

Classic Italian vegetable soup using a wide variety of vegetables, the selection depending on the region and the season. However, pasta and beans are essential ingredients.

mirepoix

Finely diced vegetables, often with the addition of bacon and herbs, fried in butter and used as a basis for sauces.

muffins

Round, flat rolls made with yeast dough and baked. In America, muffins are sweet rolls, using baking powder as a raising agent, made in special muffin pans. There are many varieties made, for instance with blueberries, raspberries, red currants or chocolate.

pie

A sweet or savoury dish baked in a pastry shell with a pastry top. It is made in a pie tin (pan) with a slanting edge 5 cm (2 in) high. The lid of dough should have a small opening in the middle so that the steam can escape, preventing the pie crust from swelling up.

ramekin or cocotte

A small, round oven-proof china or earthenware dish in which individual portions are cooked and served.

reducing

Concentrating a liquid by boiling it so that

the volume is reduced by evaporation. It increases the flavour of what is left. Strongly reducing a sauce gives a particularly tasty result with a beautiful shine.

refreshing

Dipping food, particularly vegetables, briefly in cold water after cooking to preserve the colour, mineral content and vitamins. The cooked vegetables or other items are then drained in a colander.

roasting

See baking.

roux

A mixture of butter and flour used to thicken sauces. The mixture is made by melting butter and stirring in flour. This is then diluted with milk or stock (broth) and cooked for at least 15 minutes while stirring constantly. For a dark roux, the flour is cooked until it turns brown before liquid is added. Because this reduces the thickening quality of the flour, the amount of flour should be increased.

royale

A custard-like cooked egg garnish. Milk and eggs are stirred together, seasoned, poured into small buttered moulds and poached in a bain-marie at 70–80°C (160–180°F). They are then turned out and diced.

salamander

Electric appliance used to caramelize or brown the top of certain dishes. It is comparable to a grill, which is normally used as a substitute.

sauté

Cooking food in fat in a frying pan (skillet). Small, uniform pieces of meat, fish, chopped vegetables or sliced potatoes are cooked in a pan while being tossed to prevent them sticking. In this way all sides of the food are cooked.

simmering

Cooking food in liquid over a low heat, just below boiling point. This method of cooking is often used for making soups and sauces since it makes the food tender and enables it to develop its full aroma.

soufflé

Particularly light, aerated dish made with beaten egg white which may be sweet or savoury. A meal which finishes with a mouth-watering chocolate soufflé will always be remembered with great pleasure.

soup bones

Meat bones, poultry carcass or fish bones used in making stock (broth). These are very important ingredients because they give an intense flavour to the stock (broth). Smooth beef and veal bones are ideal, but the marrow bone has the most flavour. It is important that the bones should be purchased from a reliable butcher and come from a guaranteed source so as to avoid any risk of BSE (mad cow disease).

steaming

Cooking over boiling water so that the food is out of contact with the liquid and cooks in the steam. To achieve this, the food is cooked in a perforated container over lightly boiling water or stock (broth). This method of cooking ensures that vegetables keep their flavour particularly well. They remain crisp and full of taste. Fish too can be cooked in this way without any additional fat but simply with herbs and spices. Steaming is particularly good for the preparation of low-calorie dishes for people who must follow a low-fat diet for reasons of health. But it will also appeal to everyone who loves the pure, genuine flavour of food.

stock (broth)

The flavoured liquid base of soups and sauces. Basic meat stocks (broths) for soups and sauces are made by simmering meat and bones of veal, beef, game, poultry or fish for several hours. As the liquid simmers gently, the constantly forming foam is periodically removed with a skimming ladle. When the stock (broth) has cooled down, the layer of fat can be removed so that the stock (broth) becomes light and clear. Vegetable stock (broth) is made in a similar way by boiling vegetables and herbs

straining

Filtering solid matter from liquids or draining liquids from raw or cooked food. Soups, sauces and stock (broth) are poured or pressed through a fine sieve. In the case of a stock (broth) the sieve may be lined with a coarse cloth.

string

Kitchen string is used to truss poultry or to tie a joint of meat so that it keeps its shape while being cooked.

suprême

Breast of chicken or game. The name refers to the best part of the bird, which is always prepared with the greatest care.

sweating

Frying the food lightly in a little fat in a pan over moderate heat, so that it softens but does not brown.

tartlet

Small tart made from short crust or puff pastry with a sweet or savoury filling.

tenderizing

Making tough meat tender by beating it. The meat is placed between two sheets of foil and beaten with a mallet or the bottom of a small pan until it has become thin. It is used for roulades, veal escalopes and so on.

thickening

The addition of a substance to a sauce or soup to thicken it. There are several common methods. Flour may be added and stirred continuously until the liquid thickens. A variation is to mix butter and flour as a roux to which the liquid is slowly added, again stirring constantly. Alternatively egg yolk or cream can be stirred into the liquid to make an emulsion. On no account must it be allowed to boil or it will curdle. After the yolk has been stirred into the sauce or soup, it must not be cooked any more or it will curdle.

timbale

Mould lined with pastry, blind-baked and filled with meat, fish or other ingredients in a sauce, baked in the oven or cooked in a bain-marie.

trimming

The removal of connective tissue and fat from all kind of meats. The off-cuts are used in the preparation of stock (broth) and sauces. It is important to use a very sharp knife, held flat against the meat so as not to remove too much meat in the process.

turning

Forming vegetables and potatoes into decorative shapes, such as balls, ovals or spirals. This is carried out using a small knife with a crescent-shaped blade.

zest

The thin outer rind of oranges or lemons, used for its flavour and fragrance. It is cut from the pith in thin strips, using a zester.

Herbs and spices

agar

Thickening agent made from dried algae from Asia. It is used as a vegetable gelling agent, for instance, in the manufacturing of blancmange powder, jelly or processed cheese. Agar only dissolves in very hot liquid and has highly gelatinous properties. It is therefore important to follow the instructions very carefully. It is particularly useful in vegetarian cuisine where it is an alternative to gelatine, which is made from beef bones. Agar is often combined with other thickening agents such as carob bean flour because it is very indigestible. This makes it a much more effective thickening agent.

allspice

These brown berries are grown in tropical countries, particularly Jamaica. The complex, multi-layered aroma of allspice is at its best when the fresh grains are crushed in a mortar. It is used to season lamb and beef ragouts, sausages, pies and gingerbread.

aniseed

Aniseed is often associated with the delicious aroma of Christmas cakes and pastries. The seed can be used whole, crushed or ground. It is also used in savoury dishes, for instance in the seasoning and marinades of fish and preparation of fish stock (broth). It is the main flavour of alcoholic drinks such as pastis and ouzo.

basil

Basil is undoubtedly the king of all fresh herbs used in the kitchen. It is an aromatic annual herb that plays an important part in a wide variety of dishes. It has a particular affinity with tomatoes and it is used in salads and many Mediterranean dishes.

basil, Thai

Thai basil is an important herb in Thai cuisine, used in baked noodle dishes, sauces and curries. It is available in many shops specialising in eastern food. It is very delicate and should be used as fresh as possible.

bay leaves

The leathery leaves of the bay tree have a spicy, bitter taste which becomes even stronger when dried. It is one of the ingredients of a bouquet garni. The fresh leaves are added to fish, when dried it is an important ingredient of many preserved dishes, such as braised meat marinated in vinegar and herbs, or pickled gherkins.

borage

A herb with hairy leaves and wonderful blue flowers. It has a slightly bitter, tangy taste reminiscent of cucumber and is mainly used in drinks such as Pimms. It is also a good accompaniment to salads, soups, cabbage and meat dishes.

burnet, salad

The leaves must be harvested before the plant flowers. Salad burnet is used in the same way as borage. It is only used fresh since it loses its aroma completely when dried.

caraway

Caraway is the traditional spice used in rich, fatty dishes such as roast pork, sauerkraut, raw cabbage dishes and stews – not simply for its aromatic flavour but also because of its digestive properties. It is added to some cheeses. Whole or ground, it is also used in spiced bread and cakes. Many liqueurs contain caraway because of its digestive properties.

cardamom

After saffron, cardamom is one of the most expensive spices in the world. Removed from the pod, the seeds are used ground. Just a pinch will be enough to add a delicious taste to rice dishes, cakes or gingerbread.

chervil

The fine flavour of chervil will enhance any spring or summer dish. It can be used in salads, soups and fish dishes and it is also very decorative.

chilli peppers

Red or green chilli peppers are hot and add a spicy, aromatic pungency to food. They are available fresh, dried, ground, pickled or in the form of a paste or essence (extract). When using fresh peppers, it is advisable to remove the seeds which are the hottest part. They are especially popular in Central and south-western America, the West Indies and

Asia, forming an integral part of many dishes originating in these regions.

chives

This is one of the great traditional cooking herbs which is available throughout the year. Very versatile, chives are sold fresh in bunches and are delicious with fromage frais, bread and butter, scrambled eggs or fresh asparagus. The beautiful blue flowers of the chive plant are very decorative and also delicious, making a great addition with the leaves to any salad in the summer.

cloves

The flower buds of the clove tree have an intensely spicy aroma with a bitter, woody taste. That is why it should be used sparingly. Cloves are used in marinades, red cabbage and braised dishes as well as in mulled wine and many Christmas cakes and buns.

coriander (cilantro)

Coriander seeds have been used for a long time, mainly as a pickling spice and in Oriental dishes. Fresh green coriander leaves (cilantro) have become available in many countries much more recently. Finely chopped, this sweetish spicy herb adds an exotic aroma to many dishes, including guacamole. It should be used with discretion by those who are not used to the taste.

cress

The small-leafed relative of the watercress is slightly less aromatic. It is usually sold as small plants in paper containers or as seeds to grow oneself, often with mustard as the mustard and cress used in elegant sandwiches. Cress is commonly used to garnish egg dishes and salads.

cumin

This classic spice is common in eastern cuisine and is a fundamental ingredient of curry powder and curry pastes. It adds an interesting, exotic flavour to braised dishes such as lamb, kid or beef.

curry powder

Curry powder may be made from as many as 30 spices, including among others turmeric, pepper, cumin, caraway, cloves, ginger and allspice. It is extremely versatile and in addition to its use in curries it can be used in small quantities to add flavour to many meat, fish and poultry dishes.

dill

An annual sweetish aromatic herb, common in northern European cooking but seldom used in Mediterranean dishes. The feathery leaves are used fresh in fish dishes, sauces, with fromage frais, and in vegetable dishes. Cucumber pickles (dill pickles) make use of the leaves and the seeds.

fennel

Fennel leaves have a slight flavour of aniseed and are commonly used with fish. The seeds are sometimes used to season bread. When added to fish dishes and fish stock (broth), the seeds are crushed first.

fines herbes

Classic French combination of herbs, made from parsley, tarragon, chervil, chives, and perhaps thyme, rosemary and other herbs. Fines herbes may be used fresh, dried or frozen. The commonest use is in omelettes.

galangal

A close relative of the ginger family which is much used in south-eastern cuisine. The roots can used fresh, dried, ground or dried.

garam masala

The meaning of this Indian name is 'hot mixture', and it consists of up to 13 spices. It plays an important part in the cooking of India, where it is home-made, so that its composition varies from family to family. Garam masala is available commercially in supermarkets and in shops specialising in Asian food.

garlic

Cooking without garlic is unimaginable to anyone who loves and enjoys the pleasures of the Mediterranean. Freshly chopped, it enhances salads and cold sauces, roasts, stews, braised and grilled (broiled) dishes, all benefit from the addition of garlic. Another popular use is in garlic bread.

gelatine

Gelatine is a thickening agent made from beef bones. Leaf gelatine must be soaked thoroughly in plenty of cold water for five or ten minutes before using it. It is then squeezed well and diluted in warm water. A special technique is needed when using gelatine in cream-based dishes. A few spoonfuls of cream are stirred into the gelatine. This mixture is then stirred into the rest of the cream. In this way lumps will be avoided.

ginger

The juicy roots of ginger have a sharp fruity aroma. Ginger adds an interesting, exotic touch to both savoury and sweet dishes. Because ginger freezes very well it can be kept for a long time without losing any of its flavour. A piece can be broken off whenever it is needed.

lavender

The taste of lavender is bitter and spicy. It can be used as a seasoning for lamb-based dishes, meat and fish stews and salads. The flowers are particularly decorative.

lovage

Lovage has a celery-like taste and both the stems and the leaves can be used in soup, salads and sauces. The finely chopped leaves are sometimes added to bread dumplings, and to the stuffing for breast of veal to which it adds a particularly delicate flavour.

marjoram

Sweet marjoram is a popular herb with a distinctive aroma. It can be used either fresh and dried, but like almost all herbs it is best when it is fresh. Marjoram is delicious in potato soups and omelettes. Pot marjoram is

a hardier form with a stronger flavour, so it is advisable not to use too much.

mint

Mint is delicious as mint tea and also in puddings such a mint ice cream, and in drinks. It is part of many soups, salads and meat dishes, and is often added to potatoes and peas. Mint sauce is served with lamb. Mint leaves are also often used as decoration.

mugwort

This is a variety of wormwood. It grows in the wild and the sprigs should be collected just before the plants flower. They can also be dried for later use. Mugwort is popular with roast goose and game.

mustard seeds

Mustard seeds are one of the most important ingredients in pickled vegetables such as gherkins, courgettes (zucchini), pumpkin, mixed pickles and pickled cocktail onions. They are often used too in braised beef, marinated in vinegar and herbs.

nasturtiums

Nasturtium flowers are very decorative and the leaves are delicious, their sharp, peppery taste adding a spicy touch to any salad.

nutmeg

Grated nutmeg is delicious in soups, stews, potato purée and cabbage. It is a also a traditional seasoning in Christmas cakes and confectionery. It tastes best when freshly grated.

oregano

Also known as wild marjoram, oregano is much used in Italian cuisine. It is essential in many dishes such as pizzas, pasta with tomato sauce and aubergine (egg plant) dishes. In the case of pizzas it is best to use dried oregano because the fresh leaves become brown in the very strong heat of the hot oven, thus losing much of their flavour.

parsley

The most popular of all herbs, two varieties are common, one with curly leaves and the other with smooth leaves. But it is not only the leaves that are used; the roots too are full of flavour and are delicious added to soups and sauces. Parsley has a deliciously fresh aroma and a strong taste. It is also extremely rich in vitamins and minerals, so it is an important herb for use in winter.

pepper

Black pepper and white pepper have different tastes as well as looking different. Black pepper is obtained by harvesting the unripe fruit, while white pepper is the ripe fruit which is peeled before being dried. White pepper is milder, more delicate in taste and not as sharp as black.

purslane

The green, fleshy leaves can be used raw in salads or used as a vegetable in its own right

as in the Far East. The delicious leaves have a slightly salty flavour.

rosemary

Rosemary has a particular affinity with lamb, which is often roasted with a few sprigs. It is particularly popular in France where it is used in many dishes such as soups, potatoes, vegetables, meat and fish dishes. Dried, chopped rosemary is one of the ingredients of *herbes de Provence*.

saffron

This bright orange spice is the 'golden' condiment of good cuisine, providing an inimitable flavour and colour. It consists of the dried stigmas of the saffron crocus, and about 4,000 of these are needed for 25 g (1 oz), which accounts for its high cost. But only a small amount is needed; just a few filaments or a tiny pinch of ground saffron will be enough to add a very special taste to bouillabaisse, paella or risotto.

sage

The sharp, slightly bitter taste of sage is ideal with roast goose or roast lamb. Often used in sausages, it is also one of the most important ingredients of the Italian classic 'Saltimbocca' (veal escalope with sage and Parma ham). The fresh leaves are delicious dipped in batter and fried.

savory

Savory is a peppery herb used in many bean-based dishes and also in stews and casseroles. The stem is cooked in the stew while the young shoots are chopped up and added to the dish just before the end of the cooking time.

star anise

This is the small star-shaped seed of the Chinese aniseed, native to China. The flavour is a little more bitter than aniseed itself. It can be used for baking and cooking and adds a delicious flavour to leg of lamb and dried apricots or in sweet and sour beef stew. It can also be used in puddings such as apple or quince compote.

tamarind

The pods contains a very sour juice which is much used in Indian and Thai cooking. Dishes such as baked fish with tamarind sauce, cherry tomatoes and fresh ginger are quite delicious.

tarragon

Tarragon has a delicate, spicy flavour. It can be used on its own as in tarragon vinegar or tarragon mustard, in Béarnaise as well as in a wide range of poultry and fish dishes. It is also excellent when combined with other herbs such as chervil, chives and parsley. The variety to be used is French tarragon. Russian tarragon grows easily from seed but has little flavour.

thyme

Like rosemary, this sweetish spicy herb is particularly good with Mediterranean food. It is an essential part of a bouquet garni and one of the main ingredients of *herbes de Provence*. Thyme will add a special touch to any dish, whether meat, fish, poultry or vegetables.

turmeric

Turmeric is much used in oriental cuisine. It is one of the basic ingredients of curry powder, Thai fish and meat curries and Indian rice dishes. It has an intense, yellow colour, but it should not be confused with saffron which has a very different taste.

vanilla

The fruit pods (beans) of the tropical vanilla orchid tree add a delicious aroma to cakes, puddings, ice cream, confectionery and so on. In cakes it is best to use vanilla essence (extract) while to make ice-cream and rice pudding, the crushed pod (bean) is added to the hot liquid so that it releases its delicate aroma. Vanilla sugar is made by leaving a pod (bean) in a container of sugar.

wasabi

Very sharp green radish usually available as a paste or powder. It is used to season sushi and many other Japanese dishes. It is important not to add too much. Wasabi is usually served separately as well so that every one can mix it to the sharpness they like.

watercress

Watercress grows in the wild but it should not be eaten in case it contains parasites. Cultivated watercress is readily available. This is grown in watercress beds with pure water of the correct temperature running through them. Watercress has a hot, spicy taste and is delicious on its own, on bread and butter, in green salads, in cream soups, in risottos and in potato salad.

woodruff, sweet

Smelling of new-mown hay, sweet woodruff is only available in May, and it is therefore best-known as the essential ingredient in the aromatic drinks of traditional Maytime celebrations, such as the May wine cup in Germany and May wine punch in the United States. It is delicious in desserts, such as fresh strawberries marinated in woodruff, or wine jelly with fruit and fresh woodruff.

Index

Picture acknowledgments:
The editors and publishers thank the following for their help in the creation of this book:
ADAM; Birkel; CMA; Deutsche Butter; Deutsches Teigwaren-Institut; Fuchs-Gewürze; Galbani; Informationsgemeinschaft Bananen; Knorr; Koopmans; Langguth; Maggi; Mazola; Meggle; Mondamin; National Sunflower Association; Peter Kölln, Köllnflockenwerke; Thomy Feinkost-Produkte; Uncle Ben's Impressionen Versand, Wedel: pages 117, 126

The Author:
Lena Raab works as a freelance writer and lives near Hamburg. She works mainly in the fields of cookery books and health advice.

The photographers:
Brigitte Sporrer and Alena Hrbkova met each other while training as photographers in Munich, Germany. After working as assistants to various advertising and food photographers, they now each have their own studios in Munich and Prague respectively.

The food stylist:
Hans Gerlach is a skilled cook and architect from Munich, who also works as a freelance food stylist. His clients include print and TV advertising production companies, and he also contributes his skills to cookery books.

DUMONT monte

Already published

ISBN 3-7701-7001-6

ISBN 3-7701-7004-0

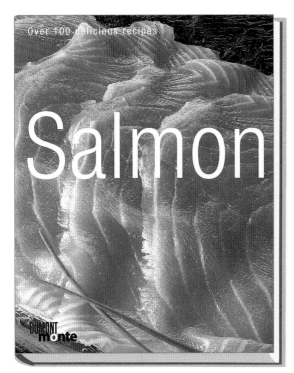

ISBN 3-7701-7002-4
(not available in USA and Canada)

Each title:
160 pages
100 colour photographs
230 x 280 mm / 9 x 11 inches
hardcover, £ 9.99 / $ 14.95

☞ **Over 100 classic and creative new recipes**
☞ **Brilliant value – a great gift buy**
☞ **Easy-to-follow methods**
☞ **100 inspirational photographs**

DUMONT monte

Already published

ISBN 3-7701-7045-8

ISBN 3-7701-7029-6

ISBN 3-7701-7003-2

Tomatoes
164 pages
over 100 colour photographs
230 x 280 mm / 9 x 11 inches
hardcover, £ 9.99 / $ 15.95

Low Fat
216 pages
over 120 colour photographs
230 x 270 mm / 9 x 11 inches
hardcover, £ 9.99 / $ 17.95

Tapas
164 pages
100 colour photographs
230 x 280 mm / 9 x 11 inches
hardcover, £ 9.99 / $ 14.95